Organic Control of
Household Pests

ORGANIC CONTROL
OF
Household Pests

Jackie French

Illustrations by Greg Jorgenson

Aird Books
MELBOURNE

Aird Books Pty Ltd
PO Box 122
Flemington, Vic. 3031
Phone (03) 376 4461

First published by Aird Books in 1988
Reprinted July 1989
Reprinted October 1989
Reprinted October 1990
Second edition 1993

National Library of Australia
Cataloguing-in-publication data

French, Jacqueline.
  Organic control of household pests.

  2nd ed.
  Includes index.
  ISBN 0 947214 47 X.

  1. Household pests – Control – Australia. 2. Natural pesticides
  – Australia. 3. Pests – Biological control – Australia. 4.
  Pesticidal plants – Australia. I. Jorgenson, Greg. II. Title.

648.7

Design by Pauline McClenahan, Captured Concepts
Edited by Betty Moore
Illustrations by Greg Jorgensen
Diagrams by Arteffect Graphics
Printed by Australian Print Group, Maryborough, Victoria

CONTENTS

INTRODUCTION

We have been indoctrinated nowadays to think of pest control as a job for experts: either pest control companies, or the manufacturers of toxic (or even carcinogenic) sprays. For many people there is no alternative: we have lost our grandparents' day-to-day expertise in household pest control.

A lot of household pest control is unnecessary; some may be vital. If there are ants in the jam and silverfish nosing round the bookcase, if there are cockroaches scuttling under the cupboards, you need to do something. But don't fall into the trap of reaching for a can of pesticide, or calling a pest control company for every stray insect that passes your way. Even in the house most insects and spiders are harmless. We are educated to hate insects, to believe that we are living in a state of siege with insects battering our defenses, while we and our loved ones survive only by buying more and more powerful and expensive commercially-prepared pesticides. We are increasingly conditioned to preventive spraying. Any insect that approaches is to be exterminated before any real pest actually appears on the horizon.

Pests need to be controlled, not eradicated. Flies, cockroaches, spiders and their like can be dangerous or spread sometimes fatal diseases. But as long as they can be kept from your food or your skin there is no need to declare all-out war, especially if the tools of battle may harm you, your family, and other species.

There is a name for pathological hatred of insects: ento-mophobia. If you know someone who suffers from it give them sympathy – but not a can of pesticide. Pesticide residues contaminate our lives enough without being added to for every scuttle under the sofa. The pesticides used in our urban areas far outweigh those used on the farms that take much of the blame for the pesticides in our lives.

The best organic pest control involves tolerance: learning to live with other species. The next step is to organise the household to minimise chances for pests to invade our lives. The two best pest control measures in the house are flyscreens and the vacuum cleaner. Screens will keep out anything from cockroaches to mosquitoes. Regular strong vacuum cleaning along shelves and in cupboards and behind books will not only clean up a lot of silverfish, fleas, cockroaches and the like but also disturb feeding areas and shelter spots to make the hidden pests in your house more visible – and easier to control mechanically, without the sprays that will harm you and your family as well as the pests.

I prefer to control the pests myself instead of calling in a pest control company. If I want to eliminate other creatures I prefer to take physical as well as moral responsibility for my actions. I know that the remedies I use will be limited, as far as possible, to the particular pests that are disturbing me, without the broad spectrum control that will affect other untargeted species. I'd rather brew my own pesticides, which are as limited in toxicity as possible and break down harmlessly. Then, any side effects will be inflicted on myself, not on Bhopal-like victims miles away, suffering from the effects of the toxic residues of substances produced so that we in the West can have our pest control done for us and shut our eyes to the side effects of both their production and their use in our homes.

Home-made pesticides are cheaper than commercial ones, you know what's in them and how long the effect will last. In the case of organic controls, this is usually only a matter of hours or days, as only substances that break down quickly are used.

This is not the place to detail horror stores of the side effects of many commercial pesticides. The aim of this book is simply to provide an alternative for concerned people, to use as they wish.

Six steps to safer pest control

1   Keep pests out

Keep the pests out of your home with screens, well-fitting doors and floor coverings. If a pest appears, work out how it got in: through a crack under a badly fitting door, for example, or through gaps in the floorboards. Some sealant around the edges of the ceiling and floor, in cracks and around door jambs will save a lot of pest control (and as a side effect improve your insulation). One useful test it to take a candle, close the doors and windows, and see how the flame flickers. Seal any gap you can find. It is remarkable how large a pest can wriggle through small spaces.

If you can't afford new flyscreens, or your window design makes flyscreening difficult, make temporary screens with second-hand mosquito netting and Blu-tak or fit 'press-ons' that can be easily unstuck when you want to open or shut a window.

When you are designing a house, think of pest prevention. Make sure kitchens are well sealed against cockroaches and rodents. Flies may come in on people's backs. If it is possible, include in your house design a 'fly antechamber': a one metre square passage between the first backdoor and the second, where flies can be brushed off.

Avoid having the kitchen right at the backdoor. Flies will linger round the door whenever they smell cooking, and make a dash for the interior whenever someone opens the door. If there is a back passage, laundry, scullery, or enclosed porch, there will be less likelihood of a fly invasion whenever you put the stewpot on.

If you have a septic system, place fly traps and repellents wherever the outflow – liquid and gas – goes. Insects are attracted to bathrooms not just by odours but by moisture as well.

2   Look for breeding places

Cockroaches can breed under mulch near the house or under black plastic or tan bark that is kept moist and undisturbed. They also like slow compost heaps – as do flies, mice and rats. Mosquitoes will breed in dog bowls that are perpetually refilled and never quite emptied, in goldfish ponds where larvae-eating fish are deceased and only pond scum remains, in permanent puddles in ferneries, and in wet saucers under pot-plants. Flies like badly sealed rubbish bins – as do cockroaches – most hen runs, dog bedding that is left damp and smelly for months at a time, and wet piles of lawn clippings left to rot around the fruit trees.

If your compost isn't heating after three days there is something wrong. Correct it before it starts to breed pests. If it is too wet, add more dry matter, cover it, or lessen the proportion of wet kitchen scraps like leftover porridge or yesterday's lasagne. Add finer materials like lawn clippings. Most of all, increase the amount of nitrogen if you've used a lot of coarse woody materials, old corn stalks or prunings or woody leaves. Add lawn clippings or diluted urine, blood and bone or liquid manure. Make this by covering green matter or manure with water and pouring it over the compost when the liquid reaches the colour of weak tea. Do this every three days till it starts to heat up. If it heats too much and either smokes or turns grey in the centre, turn it every day till it cools down. Don't leave compost hanging around. Nudge it along to decompose quickly and spread it out on your garden as soon as the original materials are no longer distinguishable.

Whatever pest you have, remember that they must have entered the house somewhere, they must have bred somewhere, they must be eating something. If you can check them at any one of these stages you will have solved your pest problem.

3   Try deterrents

Use strong-smelling or irritating substances like lavender oil or diatomaceous earth before you resort to pesticides. If you can keep clothes moths from your rugs, jumpers and curtains, it doesn't matter how many flutter about the place. If you can stop mosquitoes attacking your ankles, it doesn't matter how many are buzzing round the barbecue. Many deterrents, like lavender oil, are pleasant to have around. I keep a strong lavender potpourri by the back and front doors and it does seem to help keep out mosquitoes. Even if it didn't, I would still value the perfume whenever I entered the house.

Other deterrents, like sulphur or diatomaceous earth, will not keep your house free of spiders or cockroaches, but they will cut down the invasion to something that you may find you can live with or to numbers that can be controlled with a fly swat instead of a pest control company. Think of planting a pest control garden: one with rue and tansy and wormwood and castor oil plants, lavender hedges and feverfew clumps, grey-silver horehound and flowering elder trees, creeping mints and nut trees. Many of these are listed in Chapter 4. They can be used to make sprays and teas or may simply be useful in their own right for repelling pests from your garden and house.

4   Use mechanical means whenever possible

Vacuum cleaners are especially useful, but also try sticky strips and boards, mouse and rat traps and other traps detailed in this book. Hang fly traps outside the kitchen windows or back door where cooking smells accumulate. Keep traps permanently set for rodents, with the bait changed each week so that any invader never has time to breed. Regular vacuum cleaning, dusting and sweeping are among the best pest control measures you can use, sucking up pests and their eggs and, even better, disturbing them and their breeding places. A quick suck with the tube of a vacuum cleaner along each shelf in a bookcase each week will clean up a lot of silverfish. Regular vacuuming up and down curtains will clear up a lot of flies, especially in winter when flies shelter there in the light and warmth to re-enter the room and buzz and breed again when the weather warms up. The sudden 'fly invasion' on a sunny winter's day may just be sheltering flies coming out from behind the curtains.

5   Use specific remedies

Use baits that will attract only ants or cockroaches, for example, without wiping out other untargeted specimens. Only use the more powerful pesticides like pyrethrum or nicotine if all else fails. Insects should be cherished for their varied roles in our lives; it is very easy with broad-spectrum insecticides to kill much more than the pest you originally intended to get rid of.

6   Use only organic remedies

Use pesticides and repellents derived from natural substances that, so far, pests have shown no resistance to, and that break down quickly and harmlessly. Remember though: they will break down quickly and harmlessly. There will be no residual effect to keep killing the pests in your house. Cockroaches will re-appear if they can still fly through your windows at night. Mosquitoes will still attack your knees if they are breeding in your sodden pot plants. No organic remedy is much use without correcting the problem that led to the outbreak.

Organic remedies give you a respite, not a cure: prevention is the only sure means of pest control.

Commercial pest control products

I prefer to make my own sprays. I know what's in them; I know that no-one else will suffer side effects in making them. Better still, the effort in making them makes me consider if they're necessary. You learn to think before you squirt.

If you prefer to buy some of your pest products, always read the ingredients. Don't be reassured by labels that say 'natural' or 'ozone safe'. They may not mean much.

Which commercial products to use

Pyrethrum is a natural derivative of *Tanacetum cineriifolium*, the pyrethrum daisy. Pyrethrum paralyses insects' nervous systems. It is not harmful to humans or other mammals, unless you drink large quantities of it. You can spray it in kitchens or on vegetables you're about to pick and eat (but don't, as the spray may contain other harmful substances). Pyrethrum may, however, cause a rash in some sensitive people.

Natural pyrethrum is an extremely effective insect killer. It has a complex range of active ingredients and insects do not appear to become immune to it. It does, however, break down very quickly in sunlight and air.

Unfortunately piperonyl butoxide is often added to increase pyrethrum's efficiency. It may also combine with other more harmful ingredients and increase the risk in their use. Do not use sprays containing piperonyl butoxide near children.

Look for pure pyrethrum products. There are several on the market for both house and garden use. If you can't find what you want in the supermarket look in the garden centre. Even if a pyrethrum spray is listed for garden use, it will still be effective on other insects. *Make sure there are no other active ingredients*.

Pyrethrum sprays will kill insects; they won't keep on killing them. You need to re-apply as necessary; or better still, prevent the pest problem from recurring.

In Chapter 1, I have added notes on the hazards of commercial pesticides. Substances in those notes may be referred to as carcinogenic, mutagenic, or teratogenic.

Carcinogens cause cancer. If a substance causes or triggers cancer in a test animal it is suspected it may cause cancer in humans.

Mutagens produce changes in genetic material. This may be passed on to children. Mutagens may also cause cancer.

Teratogens cause foetuses to develop abnormally. This may cause birth defects or miscarriage.

Pyrethroids

Pyrethroids are artificial pyrethrins. They are cheaper to produce, more stable and their effects persist for longer. Like pyrethrum they have a very low toxicity to humans and other mammals, though they appear to be slightly more irritating and may provoke asthmatic attacks.

Allethrin (an early pyrethroid) and permethrin (which remains active for several weeks) are relatively safe for house use. Be careful, however, if they are combined with piperonyl butoxide – more care will be needed in spraying.

Other pyrethroids like fenpropathrin, flucythrinate, fluvinate, cypermethrin, decamethrin/deltamethrin are long lasting pyrethroid insecticides. They are more toxic than other pyrethroids and more persistent, so may affect birds, fish and soil life. They are not suitable or necessary for regular domestic use. They are however much safer than organophosphates and carbamate insecticides if you are employing a pest control company for pests like cockroaches that may need a persistent pesticide.

Pest control companies

In the past five years many companies that specialise in 'alternative' pest control have started operating throughout Australia. Look in the Yellow Pages. Several traditional pest control companies now offer safer alternatives to people who insist on them.

These changes have been brought about by public pressure. The more people who insist on safer pest control, the more changes will be made. Keep nagging.

CHAPTER 1

Household Pests

Ants

Ants tend to come indoors in dry times. Try to tolerate them. They are valuable predators, especially of fruit-fly and caterpillars. If you water more liberally outside, they may stay there or the problem may disappear when it rains. Otherwise, hunt back the ants that are coming into the house and destroy the nest outside.

Hazards of commercial pesticides

Bendiocarb is mildly toxic. Make sure it doesn't touch your skin. Symptoms include body pains, tremors, excessive sweating, headaches and a general sense of nervousness and tension. It persists for several months and can poison pets, fish and birds as well as humans.

Chlorpyrifos is an organophosphate. It is less likely to be absorbed through the skin than other organophosphates, but you still need to wear protective clothing when using it. It is toxic if swallowed. Never use pressure packs containing chlorpyrifos as you may inhale the vapour.

Prevention

There are a number of ways you can discourage ants both inside and outside the house.
- Place the legs of tables and cupboards in bottle or jar tops filled with water or oil or talcum powder to keep ants away. Top up as necessary.

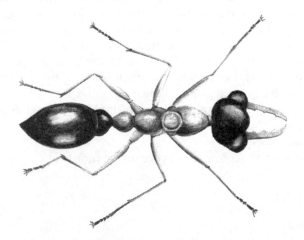

- Make sure food scraps and crumbs are kept off ant-accessible areas.
- Discourage ants in pot-plants and other garden areas by increasing the amount of humus in the soil. Add compost or mulch.
- To keep ants from trees or shrubs (where they can spread aphids and various plant diseases), place a grease band around each trunk as well as any large branches. It may be necessary to warm the grease first. Alternatively, bring to the boil 60 mL of castor oil and 150g of resin, and coat the trunk or major branches with this.
- Place pot plants on small blocks of wood to discourage ants from building nests underneath.

Repellents

Strong scents repel – at least temporarily.

I have never found the following very effective, but they might be worth trying: pennyroyal, tansy, spearmint (leaves or oil) as well as fresh catnip and fresh or dried cucumber peel. A cut lemon is also supposed to deter ants if left in their tracks. Ants vary in their tastes, habits and persistence, and repellents which fail with one lot may be effective elsewhere. The most effective repellent is probably crushed ants – especially the 'leader' larger ants. The next most effective repellent is eucalyptus oil, followed by tea tree oil.

- Leave the repellents along ant tracks.

- Tansy or mint or pennyroyal grown at doorways and under windows is also reputed to deter ants from entering a house. I have tried both with no success; but different conditions and different ants may bring more luck to others.
- Red pepper, camphor or borax on ant trails are more effective repellents. I have found a small pile of ground cloves repels small black ants – for a time.
- Sneezeweed, a pungent native shrub, is reputed to deter ants. Use either the dried leaves indoors or plant the bush near an ants' nest.
- Keep the garden round your house moist.

Control

Baits

There is a variety of baits you can make yourself if preventive measures fail. Try a bait of half-and-half borax and icing sugar. Sprinkle it along ant trails. See Chapter 3 for recipes for a wet bait, a jam bait and an effective protein bait. Any of these should be attractive to ants, though ants' tastes vary and you may need to try more than one. They should all wipe out the ant colonies eventually but, like all organic remedies, there will be no residual action and you must face the fact that the colonies may be quickly re-established.

Sprays

Any pyrethrum spray should be effective against ants. Use a home-made pyrethrum spray in a hand-pump sprayer (see Chapter 3).

Ants in paving or under the clothes line

Sprinkle talcum powder thickly. Ants dislike moving in talcum powder.

Ants under baths etc.

Drill a hole and inject pyrethrum spray. Repeat till the next is destroyed.

Destroying ants' nests

Find your ants nest by leaving out jam or peanut butter or meat baits (different ants like different baits) and following the ants back to the nest.

- Pour boiling water mixed with a little detergent down the nest. Repeat this every few days till the nest is evacuated.
- Pour a bucket of water down the nest, then spray the emerging ants with a pyrethrum spray.
- Place borax and sugar bait near the nest. Pour home-made pyrethrum spray down the nest.
- Pour a kerosene-oil emulsion down the nest (see Chapter 3). Pure kerosine can also be effective.
- Soak the nest with a pyrethrum, derris, or wormwood spray (see Chapter 3).
- Pour in half a cup of detergent and half a cup of lime in a bucket of water.

All these methods may have to be repeated several times. You may also decide to combine various methods for greater effectiveness.

New queens will establish new nests. Ant control may have to be done regularly. But if possible, tolerate them.

Cane toads

Cane toads destroy enormous numbers of native Australian animals – they are both poisonous if anything tries to eat them and will outcompete most native amphibians for food and space. If you get a chance to kill a cane toad, do: as many as possible.

Cane toads are big and 'warty' – but some native frogs are also 'warty' – and young cane toads are, of course, small. The best clue to whether or not you have a cane toad is to look for their two long, bony ridges running from between the nostrils to above the eye. Cane toad eggs, or spawn, form long gelatinous strands. If you are sure you have identified them correctly, scoop them out and leave them in the sun to dry ... and to die.

Keeping cane toads out

Cane toads dislike very dense growth. You can create a frog refuge by thickly planting around a small pond. If this isn't sufficient, build a wall around it, about 70 cm high, with gaps of about 20 cm in it. Bricks are excellent for this purpose. Cane toads won't be able to get over this fence, but many tree-dwelling frogs can; and adult cane toads won't be able to get through the 20 cm gaps, while some smaller native frogs can squeeze through.

Search your pond regularly for small cane toads, and kill them.

How to kill a cane toad

Carry a spray gun, a pump-action water pistol, or a garden sprayer filled with Dettol, and spray them thoroughly. Large numbers can be dropped in a bucket (wear gloves and sun glasses), and doused with Dettol. If you have very large quantities, fill the bucket with water, put a lid on, and very, very gently heat it till it boils. As long as the rise in temperature is gradual, the toads won't suffer.

Carpet beetles

Carpet beetle larvae will attack woollen carpets and can be mistaken for moth larvae. Carpet beetle larvae usually don't attack acrylics.

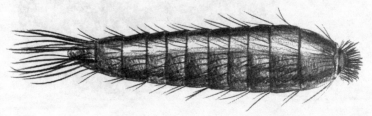

Hazards of commercial pesticides

See Moths.

Prevention

Adult carpet beetles live outdoors where pollen supplies are plentiful. Screened windows and doors will help keep carpet beetles out. Make sure carpets are regularly vacuumed and shampooed and that rugs are beaten outside. If extra control is needed, spray the carpet with a pyrethrum spray. Test a bit first to make sure it doesn't stain, especially if you are using a commercial preparations and not your own, as commercial solvents may mark the carpet.

Make sure you regularly vacuum up dead flies under the windows – they can attract carpet beetles, and pest infestations often start under windows at the edge of the room.

Cockroaches

If someone asks about pest control in the house they usually have a cockroach problem. With humans, these insects are the best adapters in the world, although they are more ancient than

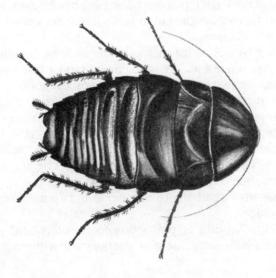

humans, and there are more of them. Don't be intimidated by cockroaches though. We are bigger.

Cockroaches are disease carriers. They may be responsible for transferring food-poisoning bacteria (salmonella), for hepatitis, diphtheria, dysentery and typhoid. They are less of a disease problem, though, than houseflies. Don't panic if you have cockroaches – if your food containers are sealed there may be no health risks.

Cockroaches have broad, flattish bodies, and broad hind legs. There are five families of cockroach in Australia. Most have wings, flat on their backs, but some native species are wingless. These rarely enter houses, preferring leaf litter and other decaying plant and vegetable matter.

Cockroaches live for up to four years, and may take from two months to a year to become mature. So far, over 400 species have been identified in Australia, though most of these aren't household pests.

Domestic pest species eat food scraps, paper and soap: rubbish or unsealed food are likely to be their main source of supply. If you have a chook or compost bucket, or a badly sealed rubbish bin, you will probably find your first roaches lurking around them. Cockroaches are usually active at night and stay undercover during the day.

Hazards of commercial pesticides

Beware of cockroach poisons containing bendiocarb: keep away from food areas. Bendiocarb is toxic. It may be a carcinogen and possible teratogen.

Dichlorvos pest strips may promote asthma. Dichlorvos is an organophosphate and depresses cholinesterase levels in the body, affecting the nervous system. Dichlorvos evaporates from pest strips and may affect people around it or food in cupboards. Dichlorvos is carcinogenic even at exposures from flea collars and pest strips. It may trigger asthmatic attacks, skin problems, convulsions. It is also associated with depression, weakness and flu-like symptoms that may be difficult to recognise. Dichlorvos kills birds, bees and fish.

Dioxacarb is a carbamate insecticide and a possible carcinogen and teratogen.

Sodium fluoride is poisonous to humans and pets; it is associated with allergenic skin reactions and asthma attacks.

Chlorpyrifos is an organophosphate, though it is less likely to be absorbed through the skin than other organophosphates. (You still need to wear protective clothing when using it.) It is toxic if swallowed. Never use pressure packs containing chlorpyrifos as you may inhale the vapour.

Pest control companies may use diaxinon. Beware of fumes. Never use diazinon in a house with children, elderly people, asthmatics or anyone with chronic illness. It persists for several months or longer in undisturbed areas in houses. Old stock may be even be more dangerous as its breakdown products are even more toxic.

In severe cases and commercial kitchens, a last resort after sealing all entrances is to use a 'pesticide bomb' containing permethrin and hydroprene. Hydroprene is a growth regulator and stops cockroaches reaching maturity to breed. Protect food and crockery from the bombs; use protective clothing, and if possible a mask.

Prevention

Organic remedies aren't long-lasting and cockroaches tend to develop resistance to long-lasting pesticides anyway. No method of killing cockroaches will control them in your house if they are continually re-infesting the place from outside. I once lived in a particularly cockroachy area of Brisbane. The flat was infested. We employed a pest control company, and had them return twice in three weeks. Then we tried another company. Nothing was effective because as soon as one lot was killed, new roaches just barged in from outside.

Prevention is the most important aspect of control; no matter how effectively you get rid of cockroaches, it will all be for nothing if they can easily return.

Install flyscreens and swinging flyscreen doors that shut automatically. Make sure doors are close-fitting. Add rubber strips at the bottom if necessary. Take a sealing gun and seal every crevice in the floors, walls, around door and window frames, etc. where cockroaches can get in. Be wary of old wooden floors under lino. They may not be cockroach proof. Get out the sealing gun again till they are. Also, check spaces behind skirting boards and ceiling fittings.

Clean up breeding sites like old piles of rubbish and slow compost heaps. Cockroaches can breed under pine chips in

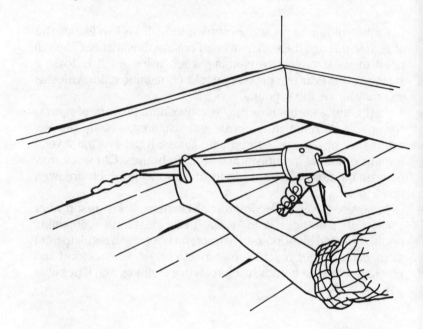

gardens and under plastic mulch. Leave baits near breeding sites and compost bins.

Make sure cupboards etc. are flush with the wall. Cockroaches are scuttlers. They prefer to cling to shelter on one or both sides. If they can't scuttle behind or under cupboards they will be more visible and more easily controlled.

Never leave food debris lying about. Though cockroaches feed on just about everything, their main food supply is domestic rubbish and debris from meals left out overnight.

Make sure all food is in sealed containers, that cupboards are cockroach proof and no food scraps or dirty dishes are left out overnight. Clean up all spilled food in cupboards – even if you think they are cockroach proof – just in case.

Make sure the lid on your rubbish bin fits tightly. Cockroaches can creep through very small openings. If the opening of your bin is at all irregular – and after a few months of bashing by garbage collectors most are – cockroaches will be able to enter and feed at will. Make sure all garbage you put in the bin is tightly sealed in garbage bags. If you dislike using plastic, place a strip of Blu-tac or plasticine around the top of your bin and press the lid firmly into it each time you replace it.

Repellents

The only really effective repellent I know is an open bottle of eucalyptus oil in the cupboard. This smells – and keeps out cockroaches. Once the smell fades the cockroaches come back in.

Take the ends of green cucumbers and leave them in any cupboard inhabited by cockroaches till the cucumbers are dry and shrivelled. This is reputed to send cockroaches away permanently. I tried it once and it wasn't effective – but then, neither were the four successive visits from two different pest control companies. Some cockroaches are persistent. Friends however have claimed the cucumbers worked for them.

Tear the leaves off a tea-tree branch and scatter them thickly in cockroach runways, near cupboards and walls and in cupboards. An open bottle of tea-tree oil is even more effective.

Control

Don't panic at finding the odd cockroach. It may have recently flown in or come with a grocery delivery. Commercial sticky cockroach traps are available. Use these to see how bad your problem is and inspect your cupboards or the area around the rubbish bin in the middle of the night.

Try a thorough sweeping in and under cupboards, under lino etc. and squash emerging roaches.

Splashes of diatomaceous earth will gradually seep into their carapaces, wearing them away. Sprinkle it in runways, next to walls, under cupboards.

Use a pyrethrum spray under logs, stones, cupboards or other breeding places (see Chapter 3).

Cockroach sealant

Use cockroach sealant in old houses where you can't seal cockroaches out. Mix 1 part borax with 2 parts flour and 1 part icing sugar. Add just enough water to make a thick dough. Knead well. Press the dough into cracks behind skirting boards and cupboards. The 'roaches will eat the dough and die. One batch of dough lasts up to a year.

Heat kills cockroaches. Close windows and doors, borrow heaters and try to get your house to 50°C for three hours. (This is done by alternative pest control companies in the United States.)

Baits

Nicotine is effective against cockroaches but should only be used as a last resort. Soak icing sugar in nicotine, place it at the bottom of a jar marked poison and put the jar near a cockroach run.

Try a bait of icing sugar and borax. Remember that baits will only work if there is no other easily accessible food. Make sure that scrap buckets and rubbish bins are sealed, no scraps or crumbs are left on benches, or bowls of peanuts on the table, and that no dirty washing-up is left on the sink.

An alternative bait is made up of half jam and half derris dust, or jam, peanut butter and derris dust.

In severe cases, sprinkle borax at the back of stoves and cupboards. This sticks to cockroaches' legs. They lick it off and it kills them.

Sprinkle borax at the bottom of rubbish bins.

Warning Borax is poisonous. Don't inhale it and keep it away from food.

Home-made cockroach trap

This does work. If you can keep more 'roaches from getting in, this – combined with rigorous hygiene – will gradually control the ones still inside. The bait is attractive to cockroaches but will be far more attractive if there is no other easily reached food.

Take an empty butter or margarine container. Fill it three-quarters full of red wine or sweet sherry. Add a dessertspoon of cooking oil. The oil will float on top of the wine, the cockroaches will climb in and drown because the floating oil will make it difficult for them to escape. You can increase the potency of this by adding some strong pyrethrum to the wine – but not if the container can be reached by pets or children.

Place the traps by your garbage bin or wherever cockroaches congregate.

Borax trap

Keep this trap out of the reach of pets and children. Place a slice of bread or potato in the middle of a saucer sprinkled thickly with borax.

Alternative trap

Take an empty, one-kilo margarine container. Grease the edges well with margarine or preferably lard: the older and smellier the better. Pour a little cooking oil into the bottom, just enough to cover it. Place a piece of cake in the bottom. Put the trap wherever you know your 'roaches congregate. They will climb down into the trap and be unable to get out.

Vanilla trap

Mix pyrethrum spray (bought or home made) with vanilla essence in a saucer. Top up as necessary.

Dust mites

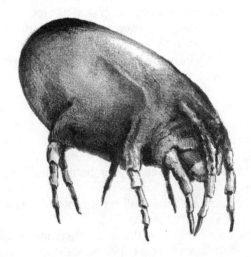

Asthma, hayfever and eczema are often at least partially due to the dust mite, *Dermatophagoides pteronyssius*, or to dust mite residues. Perhaps one in three people have some allergenic reaction to dust mites. Dust mites are tiny – just visible to the naked eye – and need warm, moist living conditions.

Dust mites may trigger an attack of asthma or eczema; they may also make it worse or predispose you to other triggers. There is some evidence that the more you can reduce dust mites the more a child's asthma will be reduced. Even if you can't rid your house entirely – and you probably can't – the more you can reduce the dust mite population, the more the asthma will respond.

As an asthmatic I've noticed that when I go into houses of other asthmatics I often start to wheeze: dust mites in the air.

Prevention

We avoid wall-to-wall carpets in our house. Instead we have tiles, cork tiles and polished wooden floors with small and large mats. These can be taken outside and hung in the sun regularly – sunlight is a good, old-fashioned dust mite control.

- Avoid long curtains that sweep the floor – and wash curtains regularly. Venetian blinds or wooden slats or plasticised fabric or oilcloth may be better in asthmatics' bedrooms.
- Vacuum mattresses regularly.
- Cover mattresses with plastic sheets; even better, cover mattresses with zippered canvas dust-coats.
- Vacuum every day, especially under beds and sofas; mop floors with a damp mop every day; mop skirtings too. Close-textured carpets can also be damp-mopped if you use discretion.
- Take all rugs outside at least once a week; beat them thoroughly, away from the house, and leave them in the sun for an hour or two.
- Avoid air-conditioning and central heating. Dust mites love central heating. There is evidence that dust mites are a worse problem since most houses began to be heated through winter – cold houses reduced populations; now they overwinter and numbers continue to grow all year round.
- In humid areas make sure your house has plenty of cross ventilation.
- Every ten days or so, take all removable blankets, mats, etc. outside in the sun for the day.
- Old houses appear to have the worst dust mite problems. If you have wooden floors (not a concrete slab) make sure they are well sealed. If necessary get a sealing gun and do it yourself. Also seal along crevices around skirting boards and cornices – any cracks where mites can accumulate and breed. This should also be done for controlling other pests, and to prevent insulation fibres or under-floor pest residues affecting anyone in the house.
- Dacron or foam rubber is best for children's toys or upholstered chairs – cut them open and change the stuffing if you can (restuffing a teddy bear may seem daunting but it's easier than it seems, even for someone who can't sew well, like me).
- Avoid feather pillows.
- Remember that there will be more mites in hot humid weather: strengthen preventative controls accordingly.

Pets

Dust mites breed in old hair and skin – both of which are shed by pets. (You may also be allergic to the pet itself.)

If you do have a pet:

- Try and restrict it to certain areas such as the kitchen, laundry, or verandah – any area without carpets which is easily swept.
- Don't let pets sit on sofas and beds. If you want them up there, cover sofas with washable blankets – and wash at least once a week.
- Be prepared for daily sweeping or vacuuming – and vacuum long curtains too.
- Brush and wash your pet regularly – outside.
- Choose 'hairy' dogs, not 'furry' ones like poodles or 'labradoodles' (a poodle labrador cross).

Dust mites and sex

Dust mites breed very rapidly on semen residues left after sex. Unromantic as it sounds, if you have asthma and enjoy sex it may be advisable to use a plastic sheet under your normal sheets, and wash it every few days. Otherwise the mattresses or mattress cover may become impregnated. The same goes for interludes on bear-skin rugs by the fire, on the sofa, or picnic blankets. If there's a wet patch, wash it.

Control

Industrial strength vacuum cleaners

These cleaners are reputed to eradicate dust mites. They don't – but they will reduce the numbers. Make sure you empty the bag outside. The stronger the vacuum cleaner the more effective it will be – but even the strongest vacuum cleaner isn't as good as sealed floors like cork tiles or sealed wood and small mats that can be beaten outside.

Room ionisers

Ionisers are said to generate charged particles – negative ions – in the air. The negative ions are said to bind particles in the air, like pollen and dust mites. If this occurs it will happen in only a very small area around the ioniser. Room ionisers appear to have little effect on allergic reactions.

Air filters

Air filters may help a lot, especially in the bedroom. The most appropriate air filters use glass fibre to trap pollens and dust and mite residues. Some air filter models with electrostatic precipitators emit ozone and can precipitate coughing fits or cause nose and eye irritation. If you are considering an air filter, hire one first to check its effectiveness.

Miticides

Miticides are effective if used correctly, though prevention must still be rigorous to avoid further build-up.

If you reorganise your house correctly, miticides shouldn't be necessary.

Earwigs

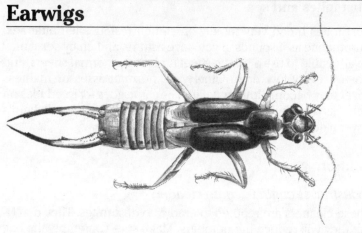

Earwigs are mostly garden pests but if numbers build up they may invade the house. Some species of earwig are more prone to housebreaking than others. Earwigs are brown to reddish-brown with thick curved pincers at the end of their bodies. Don't worry about pincers: earwigs won't bit you.

Earwigs are creepers. They like leaf litter and debris, feeding mostly on decaying plant material. They also like soft vegetables like lettuce (especially if it is turning brown) and the old leaves of dahlias and chrysanthemums. Earwigs may also eat other pests. When you see them under a damaged plant you may blame them for the damage. Don't – they are the rescuers, not the villains.

Prevention

If earwigs are a problem indoors, try to keep piles of rock, mulched garden areas and tanbark areas away from entrances to the house. Find out where earwigs are getting in – through floorboards, under doors – not because the earwigs will be more than a scuttling nuisance indoors but because where an earwig can get in, more dangerous pests like cockroaches and flies can get in too.

Control

If earwigs are really bothering you, make an earwig trap. Crumple up a piece of old newspaper, loosely. Stuff it in a flowerpot. Sprinkle it with water so it is just damp but not wet. Place it near an old wood-heap, mulched garden, or pile of garden rubbish where earwigs may breed. Change the paper every couple of days in the heat of the day. The earwigs should be sheltering there.

Alternatively, take a couple of long boards and cut grooves in them, about 6 mm wide and deep, running the length of the board. Join the two boards together so the grooves form a channel. Dampen the wood. Place it near earwig breeding spots. Shake the earwigs out every few days and stamp on them.

Soap spray kills earwigs; it also kills other species. Avoid it if you can. If you can keep earwigs off your plants, there is no need to kill them.

Ferment flies

Ferment flies are the small black specks that hover round your fruit bowl. They are sometimes mistaken for fruit-fly, but fruit-fly are unlikely to be indoors. Ferment fly feed on decaying fruit and fungus. Their activities shouldn't bother you. Keep over-ripe fruit covered and hang fly traps, but use a bait of a banana skin and an orange peel in water instead of the meat you would use in fly traps..

Fleas

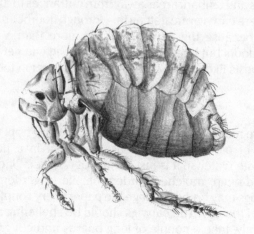

Some of Australia's 100-odd species of fleas are household fleas. They can carry a range of diseases including bubonic plague and murine typhus. Dog fleas are a different species (human fleas are *Pulex irritans*, dog fleas *Ctenocephalides*) but most fleas are found on a variety of hosts (see under 'Pets' in Chapter 2). If fleas' preferred food isn't around, they may move to another host nearby. Flea problems in Australia are usually from cat or dog fleas. It is unusual for them to jump straight from cat or dog to human. More commonly it will be from cat or dog to carpets, rugs, etc. and then onto anyone around. A flea repellent wash for a pet may mean fleas on humans the next day.

Fleas can live for 125 days without food and this is one reason why they appear to infest empty houses. Flea pupae need vibration to stimulate them to leave their cocoons: the sort of vibration you get when a previously empty house is inhabited again.

Flea eggs look like castor sugar: small white granules. The larvae are slim white maggots, usually less than 10 mm long. The larvae don't suck blood like the adults. They feed on skin scale and other plant and animal debris.

Flea bites are red and hard and usually appear on legs but may be all over the body if they have infested a bed you have been sleeping in. You may also have a feeling of a hopping itch.

Hazards of commercial pesticides

Flea powders, washes and collars may affect young children who play with pets, or who play on the lawn or carpet where these have been used.

Bendiocarb is mildly toxic. Make sure it doesn't touch your skin. Symptoms include body pains, tremors, excessive sweating, headaches and a general sense of nervousness and tension. Bendiocarb persists for several months and can poison pets, fish and birds as well as humans.

Diazinon may be used in flea collars. Diazinon is toxic to birds, bees and fish. It has caused birth defects in animal tests.

Lindane has been associated with the often fatal aplastic anaemia. Lindane is highly toxic.

Maldison is one of the safest organophosphates, but it has been associated with possible miscarriages or birth deformities. It will kill earthworms.

Carbaryl is an ingredient in many flea collars and flea shampoos. It can be absorbed through the skin and is poisonous. It kills earthworms (don't wash your pet on the lawn) bees, fish and some shellfish.

Flea collars may contain dichlorvos. Dichlorvos may trigger asthma. It is an organophosphate and depresses cholinesterase levels in the body, affecting the nervous system. The dichlorvos evaporates from pest strips and may affect people around it or food in cupboards. It is carcinogenic even at exposures from flea collars and pest strips. It may trigger asthmatic attacks, skin problems, or convulsions. It is also associated with depression, weakness and flu-like symptoms that may be difficult to recognise. Dichlorvos kills birds, bees and fish.

Prevention and control

Hard and constant vacuuming is the best control measure for fleas. Vacuum up and down curtains at least once a day, along sofas, cushions, beds and all possible crevices. Take cushions and unused mattresses outside and sun them for a day. Vacuum them before you bring them back inside.

Allow at least several hours for 'flea vacuuming' if there is a flea plague. There is no point doing one room one day and another the next. You will just be leaving a source of infection for the rest of the house. Sprinkle lavender oil liberally around the house, on carpets and curtains, etc. once you have vacuumed.

Make sure that you have controlled fleas on any domestic pets you have (see Chapter 2).

If you find a flea, either squash it with your fingernails or drown it in a bowl of water, with a little oil on top so the flea can't crawl out.

Long dishes of water will trap fleas, and flyscreens will help prevent entry.

An old bush remedy for fleas in the bed was to bring a young lamb inside and put it in the bed before you got into it. The fleas would jump onto the lamb which was then put outside. Other remedies included hanging blankets over a fence and repeatedly pouring boiling water onto them, or draping flea-infested fabrics and carpets over ants' nests so the ants ate the fleas. You then got rid of the ants.

In severe cases, spray the house liberally with pyrethrum spray. Make sure all windows and doors are shut and pay special attention to carpets, curtains, rugs, sofas, animal and human bedding, and any odd corners where scales of skin and human hair might accumulate: under beds and dressing tables or under bathroom cupboards. Go out visiting and come back a few hours later. Commercial pyrethroid and bombs can also be used.

Test the spray on materials first, especially if you are using a commercial spray: solvents and other ingredients may stain carpets or furniture covers.

Wormwood spray will also kill fleas, though it breaks down quickly and seems to have no residual effect.

Fleas are often associated with pets. See 'Pets' for flea powder and flea washes.

Flies

There are 200 species of flies in Australia. The major pests are the common housefly and the bush fly.

Hazards of commercial pesticides

Dichlorvos may provoke asthma. It is an organophosphate and depresses cholinesterase levels in the body, affecting the nervous system. The dichlorvos evaporates from pest strips and may affect people around it or food in cupboards. It is carcinogenic even at exposures from pest strips. It may trigger asthmatic attacks, skin problems, convulsions. It is associated with depression, weakness and flu-like symptoms that may be difficult to recognise. Dichlorvos kills birds, bees and fish.

Tetramethrin is a synthetic pyrethroid which acts extremely quickly. It is toxic to fish but has a low toxicity to humans. It is relatively safe but associated with asthma attacks. Allethrin is another, relatively safe pyrethrin. Both break down quickly in light. A pure pyrethrum spray, however, is safer, though not as fast-acting or long-lasting.

Permethrin is the most long acting of the pyrethroids and may still be poisonous weeks later. Avoid it – you don't need a long-lasting spray to control flies.

Dimethoate is often used in fly sprays to be used outside or in large areas. It is possibly carcinogenic; it has been shown to be mutogenic and teratogenic in animal tests. If you must use it wear a respirator and overalls. Better still, don't use it.

Houseflies

Houseflies spread disease and need to be controlled.

The housefly is seldom away from houses or domesticated-animal shelters. Houseflies try to get inside – bush flies try to get out. Most of your houseflies probably breed near the house. The only way to control them is to clean up compost heaps, lawn clippings etc. – anything that's rotting. The fly is between 6.5 and 7.5 mm long with a striped abdomen. It feeds on decaying plant and animal matter and faeces. It is most active during the day and loves to shelter indoors.

Female flies lay up to 120 eggs that hatch into fat, white to yellow maggots. Housefly eggs take 12 to 24 hours to develop. These mature in four to seven days (more in cold weather), then pupate in the soil. Flies usually only live a few weeks but can live much longer in cold weather, and flies have been known to 'overwinter' behind curtains and emerge to breed when the weather warms up.

A housefly can fly seven kilometres a day and will travel 15 kilometres in search of food. Houseflies carry bacteria on their hairy bodies, and regurgitate fluid from their crop. They may also be responsible for the spread of salmonella, poultry tapeworm,

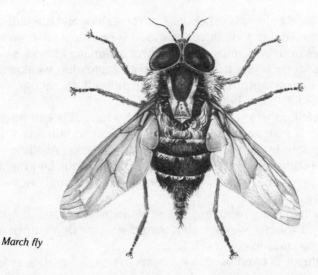

March fly

parasitic worms, tuberculosis, cholera, typhoid fever, polio, and gastroenteritis. Flies in slaughterhouses have shown high levels of contamination that persists from the maggot stage to the fly stage and salmonella have been recovered from tagged flies more than five miles from the original point of infection.

Bush flies

These are smaller than houseflies and are widespread over all of Australia, though they are more common in dry areas. They are rarely seen inside, and stop flying at night. Bush flies disappear with the first frost. They have an annoying habit of resting on backs and faces. Female bush flies are after the protein from your sweat, tears, blood and saliva. The smaller the bush fly, the more protein they need.

Repellents that work with other flies are less effective with bush flies, and even brushing them with your hand may fail to disturb them for long. Most bush flies breed in manure, not your garbage bin. It is hoped that they are being gradually controlled by CSIRO's ill-funded dung beetle program. Bush flies are blown into cities on the wind. In Sydney and Melbourne this is usually in spring. If bush flies bother you, pester the Federal Government for more CSIRO funding for dung beetles – it's a better long-term option than fly spray.

Bush flies can transmit trachoma and contagious ophthalmia.

March flies

These are horseflies (*Tabanus*), with large eyes and bodies and powerful wings. The females lay their eggs near water, often on the leaves of overhanging reeds. Larvae drop into the water or mud to complete development. Only female march flies suck blood. They are most active in summer, and especially prevalent in coastal areas and timbered valleys and mountain ranges.

Prevention

Flyscreens and swinging flyscreen doors are a necessity to keep flies away. Make sure doors are well-sealed with no gaps underneath, especially in the kitchen where attractive cooking smells will seep out. If flies are coming in, trace them to their source, then block it up. In bad fly areas you might consider an 'airlock' – a closed area between two doors as an entry to the kitchen – where flies can be removed from people's backs before entering the second door. Flies commonly enter houses on people.

Flies may come down the chimney in summer. Block it up with a sliding piece of board that can be removed easily when you light the fire. Unfortunately, the updraught and warmth of a fireplace makes the chimney an attractive point of entry for flies.

Sudden infestations near your house may mean that flies are breeding nearby. Check rubbish bins, both yours and the neighbours'. Buying them a new, well-sealed rubbish bin may be a cheap way of getting rid of flies. Wrap scraps well before you put them into bins. Check also hen houses, septic outlets, damp dog-bedding and slow compost heaps. Throw away the dog's left-over dinner. Don't leave lawn clippings in a pile. Clean the barbecue.

Repellents

Mint, tansy or basil growing round the door are supposed to keep flies from the kitchen; I have never found them to work. Pennyroyal oil brushed into the wood around benches does seem to keep them away – except when there is something more odorous and attractive, like meat, on the bench.

Flies do stay away from walnut trees with layers of decaying walnut leaves below them. Plant walnut trees outside your window. They are deciduous, so they are good for mitigating climatic extremes too. Other nut trees are also reputed to be fly repellent, though not as effective as walnuts. Be warned though: you need many years of leaf accumulation for any effect.

If for some reason a door must be kept open, a jet of cold air forced across it will keep flies from entering.

Flies round your eyes

The flies that gather on you are probably bush flies. Wear a big hat – bush flies don't like the 'indoors' and won't come into the shade of your hat.

Peppermint oil with citronella oil or pennyroyal oil rubbed on your skin will repel flies somewhat, as will full-strength eucalyptus oil, crushed mint or native peppermint or – at a pinch – crushed stinking roger, though the latter should be used with caution as people with sensitive skin may develop a rash. Of all these, eucalyptus oil is the most effective.

An old farmer's remedy for restless cows involves crushing mint leaves and rubbing them around the rear of the cow to repel flies that may be upsetting her. A Central European trick was to plant fly-repelling rue around manure piles and barn entrances to inhibit flies breeding there. An old-fashioned way of preventing meat from becoming flyblown was to rub it thoroughly with fresh rue. Rue is poisonous, however, and covering the meat with a small flyscreen is a better solution.

Spiders, many birds – especially swallows by the house – dung beetles and other dung decomposers, frogs, toads, lizards, and ants are all fly predators.

Control

The best fly control is a fly swat. Check along windows and the window-sides of curtains each morning. Any flies around should congregate there for heat and light. They will be relatively slow moving in the morning and accordingly easier targets. Make this a regular patrol.

The long, sticky fly-trapping ribbons used in my childhood are still available. They do keep numbers down if you don't mind a string of fly corpses in the room. Imitate these by spreading a mixture of glue and molasses on a piece of yellow board or cardboard.

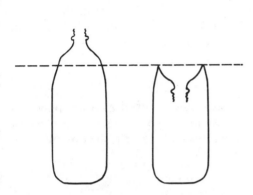

Cut the top off a plastic bottle at the shoulder. Turn it upside down and tape it into the bottle. Half fill the bottle with water, add a few drops of oil, and drop in some meat. Hang this trap near the kitchen door, the windows, or wherever else flies gather or may enter the house.

A *light trap* can be made to catch indoor flies at night. Attach a funnel to an old cream bottle. Hang the funnel under a light in an unused room, and leave the light on during the night. Flies will be attracted to it and fall down the funnel.

Fly traps

There are several baited fly traps available commercially. Most are very effective, but effectiveness depends on the bait. If one bait fails, try another. Home-made fly traps are cheap and simple to make.

Sprays

Home-made pyrethrum spray may be used as a fly spray (see Chapter 3). Check first that no-one in your household is sensitive to it. Rub a little on the inner arms and see if a rash develops. Keep out of reach of children.

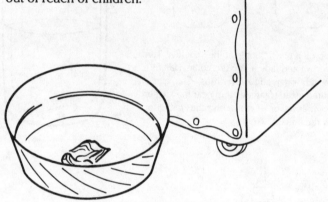

Dish trap Place a dish of meat and pyrethrum spray in an inconspicuous place. The meat will not smell if covered by liquid.

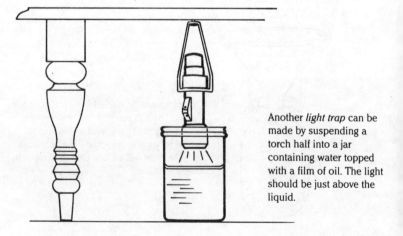

Another *light trap* can be made by suspending a torch half into a jar containing water topped with a film of oil. The light should be just above the liquid.

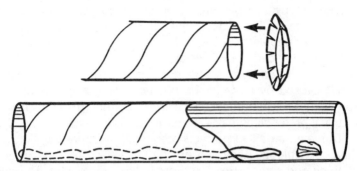

Cylinder trap Use the cardboard cylinder from an empty gladwrap, aluminium foil, or kitchen paper roll. Seal one end with a cardboard "cap", using sticky tape. Place some meat inside and line the bottom with a thick layer of clag paste. Flies will get stuck in the paste.

Lice and nits

Lice are tiny, wingless, and hairy, usually with wide claws. They feed by sucking blood. The eggs are called nits. Lice are very specialised: many are restricted to one sort of host or even to a particular part of that host. For example, *Pediculus humanus* lives only in human hair, while *Pthirus pubis* can survive only in pubic hair.

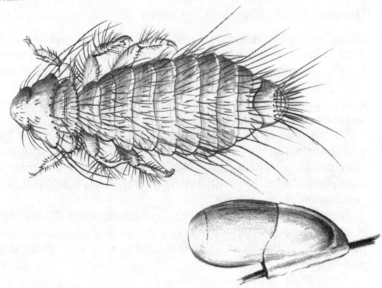

Lice are usually passed on by direct contact. Variations in temperature kill lice as does light. Lice can sometimes be passed on in other people's combs, hats, etc., but close contact is more likely to be the cause. Bird lice are usually biting lice. Only sucking lice are found on humans. So, contrary to myth, lice infestations aren't caused by birds in the rafters. (Mites, however, can be spread by birds to humans.) Lice aren't a symptom of dirty hair. In fact, lice prefer clean hair – it's easier to hold on to.

The lice that affect humans are small, puncture the skin and then suck blood. Body lice are pinhead-sized and lay eggs in clothing and sheets. Head and pubic lice are smaller. The eggs (nits) attach to hair. It takes about nine days for lice eggs to hatch and about another nine days for them to become mature. Lice are most common in overcrowded conditions as they are spread by close contact. Pubic lice are usually transferred during sex.

Symptoms

The main symptom is itching, though scratching can irritate the area and blisters, crusty sores or scratch lines may form. In the hair, nits are grey-coloured eggs attached to the hair near the scalp. They are clearly visible with a magnifying glass, just visible without one. In pubic hair, the lice look like tiny scabs and can be seen partially buried in the hair follicles. These become inflamed and may develop pus-filled pimples.

Hazards of commercial pesticides

Lindane is readily absorbed through the skin. It is associated with bone marrow disorders like aplastic anaemia and leukemia; there have been cases of central nervous system toxicity after its use in shampoos. It is cumulative, stored in fatty tissues, and may cause liver and kidney tumours. It is a possible carcinogen. Never use lindane on young children.

Chlorpyrifos is an organophosphate. It is less likely to be absorbed through the skin than other organophosphates, but you still need to wear protective clothing when using it. It is toxic if swallowed. Never use pressure packs containing chlorpyrifos as you may inhale the vapour.

Benzyl benzoate may be absorbed through the skin. Bioallethrin is a synthetic pyrethroid. Washes containing bioallethrin are probably safe. Malathion should be used with protective clothing and respirators – not used on your hair. Overdose symptoms include sweating, muscular weakness, tremors and nausea. Malathion has not been proved safe to use during pregnancy.

At least one head wash for lice contains pyrethrum. This is much safer than the other commercially available washes, though allergic reactions are possible. Use other measures first.

Control

Frequent bathing in hot, very soapy water may be enough to control lice. Rinse hair with 1 part vinegar and 3 parts water. This will help unstick the eggs from the hair. This is not enough to control a bad case of nits – but daily washing in a nit plague may be enough to give you some protection. Comb hair regularly with a very fine comb.

Comb thyme oil or rosemary oil through the hair. If this isn't easily available commercially, you can make your own if you have fresh herbs. This *may* kill nits, though it usually isn't a sufficient control. It will, however, make nits easier to remove. Divide hair into strands in good light, and strip each strand with long fingernails or tweezers. Do this daily till no eggs have been seen for three days. This takes time – and more effective remedies are available.

There are now several pyrethroid-based lotions commercially available. When used according to directions, they are both safe and effective.

Old-fashioned remedies include kerosene (which is dangerous and carcinogenic), olive oil combed through the hair, or a quassia infusion. This used to be available from chemists but I have not been able to find one that stocks it now. Some mail order nurseries, including Phoenix Seeds in Tasmania, supply it for garden pest control. Quassia spray is an old-fashioned nit remover. It is a weak, general insecticide and can be made quite easily at home. It may be effective.

Two other controls are electric 'lice combs' and a mixture of 1 part tea tree oil to 3 parts olive oil. the latter is rubbed through the hair and left overnight. The former 'electrocutes' the lice. I haven't yet tried either, but I have heard good as well as bad reports on both.

Remember that eyebrows can harbour lice. Suffocate them by rubbing in petroleum jelly and leaving overnight.

Note: If a secondary infection follows irritated lice bites, seek medical attention.

Millipedes

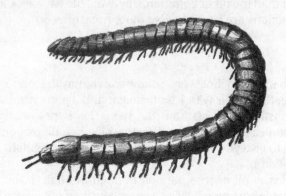

Millipedes are long, thin, hard and shiny, with many paired legs. They vary in colour, but most problem ones are brown or black. They tend to curl up when scared.

Millipedes may breed in large amounts of organic matter in the garden. They can hollow out strawberries and may attack young roots and seedlings, but usually they don't cause much damage.

The black Portuguese millipede, *Ommatoiulus moreletii*, is the main household pest millipede. They don't damage the garden, but will happily wander through the house – often in large numbers. They don't cause any damage, but do tend to worry people, especially if they are mistaken for scorpions or the householder has a low 'creepy-crawlie tolerance'. They also stink if you squash them.

The best way to get rid of millipedes in the house is to sweep them up. This is less work and less ecologically destructive than spraying them. It is even better to keep them out altogether. A good temporary barrier is a sprinkle of talcum powder around the house, expecially near doorways and French windows. A permanent structure can be made by surrounding the house with a short metal barrier. It should be bent over at the top, with the bend facing outwards, so that the millipedes can't climb up and over.

Mosquitoes

So far, over 200 species of mosquito have been described in Australia. Some mosquitoes are active during the day, some at night, while some are active at any time. Most mosquitoes will attack any warm-blooded animal. Some species even attack reptiles. Only female mosquitoes suck blood. The males are thinner and have hairy-looking antennae. They feed on sap and nectar, using the piercing and sucking techniques that the females use for blood.

Some mosquitoes have only one host, like birds or reptiles. Others aren't so selective. Most mosquitoes are active at night, though dark, moist places may have active mosquitoes during the day.

Mosquito larvae always need moisture. A small puddle is enough, or a damp fernery. A common breeding place for mosquitoes in the suburbs is the dog's bowl: often refilled, never entirely emptied. Goldfish ponds without the goldfish (which eat mosquito larvae), puddles on tank tops or stagnant pools in shrubberies are also likely breeding places.

The most common household mosquito pests are the brown house mosquito, the common banded mosquito, and the salt marsh mosquito. The most widely distributed is the *anophelene* mosquito, ranging from Victoria to North Queensland. Various mosquitoes in Australia are capable of carrying diseases like malaria, filariasis, dengue, and Murray Valley encephalitis.

Hazards of commercial pesticides

See under 'Flies'.

Prevention

Mosquito nets and flyscreens on windows and doors are the best mosquito controls. If you can't afford flyscreens, try to buy secondhand mosquito netting and pin it up.

Encourage predators: dragonflies, toads, tadpoles, frogs, goldfish and other fish, and birds (especially swallows) eat large quantities of mosquitoes and their larvae. In some parts of Asia dragonflies larvae are routinely placed in all water containers.

Clean up breeding areas around the house. Get rid of stagnant water wherever possible. This includes tanks, dog dishes that are topped up instead of emptied, fish ponds, and tyres around fruit trees that may collect water inside. (We once used old tyres round fruit trees, then found we were suddenly getting mosquitoes. They were breeding in the stagnant water collected in the old tyres. Holes drilled in the tyres let out the water.) If the water is too valuable to remove, add a film of oil to it (use vegetable oil for drinking water) or cover with mosquito netting. Alternatively, add goldfish.

Grow casuarina trees or willows or melaleucas in wet, boggy areas to drain the surplus water. Install drains. If you have permanent water around, like a dam, stock it with fish to eat the mosquito larvae.

Repellents.

See page 91 for home-made rub-on repellents.

Lavender oil seems to be the most effective repellent. Apply the oil every two hours for women and every four hours for men. The oil can be diluted with olive or other oil to make it spread further; but it should remain fragrant. Lavender-scented clothing will also repel mosquitoes. In the garden, branches of lavender can be rubbed on face and hands. Remember that if *you* can't smell lavender, the mosquitoes won't be repelled.

An excellent mosquito repellent is 1 part methylated spirits, 1 part lavender oil, 1 part eucalyptus oil, and 1 part cider vinegar. Add 1 part pennyroyal oil if you can find it.

Sassafras oil, citronella oil or pennyroyal oil rubbed on the skin will also repel mosquitoes, though less effectively than the repellents above. American pennyroyal (*Hedeoma pulegioides*), is supposed to be more effective than the European pennyroyal (*Mentha pulegium*). Citronella oil may also attract oriental fruit-fly. This may not bother you but probably the oil shouldn't be worn when picnicking under a ripening apricot tree.

Candles containing citronella oil are sometimes available commercially and can be burned as mosquito repellents. They are only slightly effective, repelling mosquitoes wherever the scent flows. Unfortunately, as heat and smoke rise, the repellent may not be working where you want it – on your legs – repelling mosquitoes perfectly on the ceiling or in the tree tops instead.

Lavender-scented candles could be made at home. Melt commercial candles in a saucepan, add lavender oil till the whole is strongly perfumed, then re-mould around the wick. Alternatively, melt one candle, add lavender oil, then dip other candles in the melted wax so they have a thick coating of lavender-scented material. This is more effective if you add dried powdered wormwood and dried powdered pyrethrum flowers. Both burn if they are quite dry. You can also add a little salt petre for added flare.

An extract of the castor-oil plant is marketed as an organic mosquito repellent in the USA. Use the powdered or freshly-crushed leaves if you have a plant. Castor-oil plants can also be planted round the garden to help keep it free from mosquitoes.

The leaves of molasses grass and sassafras are also reputed to be effective mosquito repellents if rubbed on the skin.

Two traditional mosquito repellents are fat and mud plastered on the skin, and smoky fires, preferably with green eucalyptus leaves. This may be a last resort at a barbecue.

Home-made mosquito 'coils'

Dry as many of the following as you possibly can: lavender flowers, wormwood leaves, castor-oil plant leaves, pennyroyal leaves, cedronella leaves, pyrethrum or feverfew flowers. Lavender and wormwood are essential.

Place one cup of dried leaves in a can. Add a dessertspoon full of derris dust (unless you have added at least one-quarter of a cup of pyrethrum or feverfew flowers). Add a few drops of lavender oil, and pennyroyal oil, citronella oil or paperbark oil if you have them. Add the wax of three melted candles; dip in one of the wicks. Two or three candles may be needed to keep an area mosquito free.

Control

Home-made pyrethrum fly spray will kill mosquitoes and their larvae if sprayed around the room. I have heard that 'dipel' is also effective against mosquito larvae but I have been unable to confirm it. (Tadpoles clean up the mosquito larvae around here before I can get to them first.)

Moths – clothes

There are over 140 species of clothes moths in Australia. Most are an insignificant grey or white: very hard to notice till you see the holes left by their larvae. Clothes moths lay eggs singly or in groups. The eggs hatch in about a week. The larvae are about 10 mm long and feed for up to 65 days before they pupate.

Clothes moth larvae feed on all woollen materials including carpets, blankets, upholstery and furniture. They also eat linen, felt and cotton and even synthetic materials if they are contaminated by perspiration or urine.

Hazards of commercial pesticides

Dichlorvos pest strips may induce asthma – never hang them in wardrobes. Dichlorvos is an organophosphate and depresses cholinesterase levels in the body, affecting the nervous system. The dichlorvos evaporates from pest strips and may affect people or food in cupboards. It is carcinogenic even at exposures from flea collars and pest strips. It may trigger asthmatic attacks, skin problems, convulsions. It also causes depression, weakness and flu-like symptoms that may be difficult to recognise. It kills birds, bees and fish.

Napthalene has been associated with pernicious anaemia and has been associated with haemolytic anaemia in very young children. It is also poisonous. Another hazard with napthalene is that it may not be effective.

Camphor is poisonous if swallowed. Keep out of reach of children. Even the vapour may affect a young child, though not in amounts usually found in cupboards or lingering on clothing. Use with caution.

Prevention

Given that you'll either be wearing or closely living with the grubs' food supply, spraying them with poisons means you will have to live with that too. It is unnecessary. Repellents will keep clothes moths away from your fabrics. Washing or dry cleaning will kill the larvae. Sealing clothes or blankets, that may be infected with moths' eggs, in plastic bags and putting them out into the sun for a day will control infestations. Where time is limited, cupboards can be fumigated with a pyrethrum spray, but this should be used as a last resort. *Never* store clothes that smell of old sweat. Wash them first. Store valuable clothes in plastic or linen bags that moths can't get into to lay their eggs.

Repellents

Remember that clothes moths are attracted to the smell of humans. If you can cover up the 'human scent' you won't attract moths.

Almost *any* scent will do. I like perfume oils like oak moss and magnolia – but the stuff that Aunt Doris gave you for Christmas will do as well. Try to find a scent you like to live with.

The classic moth repellent is lavender. Lavender sachets kept with your clothes, or lavender oil or water sprinkled onto your woollens when you put them away for the winter, not only makes them fragrant but reasonably mothproof. If it doesn't you need more or fresher lavender. Cotton 'lavender' or santolina and the Tasmanian or Bridgeport oil cultivar (ask for them at specialist nurseries) appear to be most effective. Both the leaves and flowers can be used, but the leaves don't have the perfume strength or oil content of the flowers, so use more of them.

Other moth repellents include dried mint or dried southernwood or wormwood, waterpepper, and white cedar leaves. These can also be used in combination with lavender. Spanish farmers used to pack their lambs' fleeces for sale with layers of southernwood to keep away the moths. Southernwood also repels many other insects. Bay leaves or neem tree or tobacco leaves can also be used, especially in combination with other repellents. I also use camphor mint and vanilla grass. The latter become more fragrant as they get older and dryer, and will scent clothes all winter.

Mugwort used to be widely used in medieval England as a moth repellent but is little used today, possibly because now hops have replaced mugwort in beer the herb is less well-known. Mugwort flower buds should be picked just before they open, then dried and used whole. The leaves can also be dried and used as moth repellents.

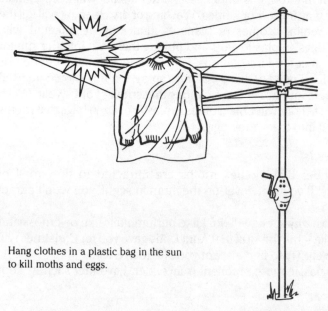

Hang clothes in a plastic bag in the sun
to kill moths and eggs.

Add either flowers or leaves to any potpourri, or sprinkle mugwort leaves or dried flowers in between blankets or other woollens in storage.

Rosemary is mentioned in an 11th century herbal guide as a moth repellent for use in clothes chests. There is no need to dry rosemary before use. Just pick branches and store in drawers and cupboards. It can also be added to herb sachets.

Woodruff is a sweet-scented old 'strewing herb' for scattering among clothes, linen and rugs to keep away moths. Its scent is like new hay and its active constituent, cumarin, is highest in spring when woodruff flowers. Pick both flowers and leaves just before or during flowering. The scent is strongest after the leaves and flowers have been half-dried. Woodruff should always be dried at a low temperature to keep its colour and perfume. Make sure any repellent you use has a strong scent. If it hasn't it is unlikely to be effective.

Moth bags and sachets make effective repellents that last for up to six months. Mix equal quantities of dried lavender leaves or santolina with dried tansy or costamary leaves. Chop them finely together and place them in a bag. Add some pyrethrum flowers to increase their effectiveness. A number of repellent sachets are listed in Chapter 3.

Moths dislike cloves. A clove-studded orange, lemon or lime pomander in your cupboard will repel insects and keep clothes smelling fresh. Take a fresh, firm-skinned orange, lemon, lime or grapefruit. Push in as many cloves as possible, wrap it in tissue paper and then leave it for a couple of weeks. Take it out, tie a ribbon around it and hang it in the cupboard or place it in a drawer. Apples also make sweet-smelling pomanders, though these tend to shrink more than citrus ones. You can also just scatter a liberal amount of dried cloves with your clothes – or dried garlic, if you don't mind your woollens smelling like yesterday's salad.

Add a dash of lavender-oil to the final rinse as you wash your woollens. Use a little water and as much lavender oil as possible for this rinse. Equal parts lavender oil and eucalyptus oil will also soften woollens. If you don't have easy access to lavender oil, fill a large pot with lavender leaves and flowers. Half fill with water, put on a lid and bring to the boil. Take off the heat and let steep till cool. Strain and don't dilute. Use this liquid to rinse your clothes – don't store it though – it soon goes bad. Wormwood can also be used in the same way; but wormwood smells unpleasant to most people as well as to moths and will give an unpleasant, almost sweaty odour to your clothes.

Woollen carpets

Most carpets are treated with insecticide when they are made. Unless you have hand-made carpets there is no need to worry about preventing insect attack till you see the symptoms. Rugs should be taken outside and shaken at least once a week – more if there has been previous damage – and left in the sun for an hour. Carpets should be vacuumed at least once a week and shampooed regularly. This should normally be enough to prevent pest damage. Pieces of dried or fresh lavender placed under woollen carpets at regular intervals should protect it from moth damage for up to five years, depending on the strength of the lavender you are using. If you can no longer smell the lavender from about a metre away it probably needs replacing.

Moths – food moths, weevils, and beetles

There is a wide range of stored-food pests, including grain and meal moths, warehouse moth, rice weevil, grain beetle and others. Weevils in flour or flour products like biscuits and cereals, and in other grains or beans, are a pest: such food may be 'webbed' together.

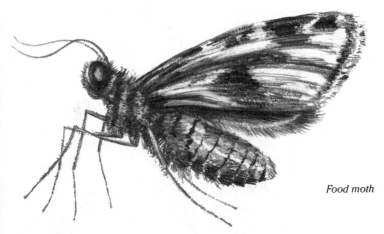

Food moth

Prevention

Never buy packets with 'webby' bottoms. You may be introducing pests on legs. Always transfer the contents of packets to sealed jars when you get home. Often debris in warehouses or cartons attracts – pests – and their eggs or larvae may cling to the bottom of the packets you bring home.

Freezing packets overnight or placing them on high in the microwave for 10 seconds will kill pests.

Make sure all food is kept in sealed jars. Clean cupboards regularly and don't leave unsealed packets around.

Commercially prepared food can be kept weevil-free by storing it in vacuum-sealed containers or creating a vacuum with dry ice. An old-fashioned way of imitating this at home was to keep food in airtight drums with room left at the top for a candle. The candle was lit before the lid was put on. When the flame had used up all the oxygen the candle would go out and the drum should have been reasonably airless.

If food is pest-free when you get it and is kept sealed and away from breeding areas when it is temporarily opened, food pests shouldn't be a problem.

Clean up all spilled foods, especially cereals and crumbs as these can be breeding spots. Don't stick them in the household compost bucket or an inside garbage bin, as any eggs may hatch before the contents are disposed of. Even sealing them in a plastic bag isn't foolproof as many pests can fit through 2 mm openings. Feeding them to the chooks is safe, as are outdoor bins, or soaking the infected food in water for about two weeks.

Repellents

Chopped garlic, slightly dried in the oven and placed in a paper bag, will help deter moths, and surprisingly, the smell doesn't taint dry food. Don't use it with moist food, however. Bay leaves placed throughout storage jars are also effective moth repellents as are sassafras leaves. Like garlic, the latter should be placed in a paper bag before storing with food.

An old-fashioned way of storing dried fruit involved packing it between layers of lavender leaves or bay leaves.

Weevil

Make a weevil sachet. Separate a bulb of garlic into cloves. Don't bother to peel them. Place them on a greased tray in a slow oven for an hour, or in the warming drawer of a slow-combustion stove overnight.

Take fresh bay leaves or still-fragrant dry ones. Crush them. Wrap the leaves and garlic together in a bit of thin cloth – old sheet, butter muslin, etc. – and store with food. Always keep several of these in any cupboard where food is stored even if you are sure there is no spilled debris. If you are storing large quantities of food you will need a sachet for every 6 cm of food.

Control

Food moth trap
Take some old oil in which you have fried food, or if you never fry, heat up a cupful of oil with a spoonful of breadcrumbs till they turn dark brown. Place in an open jar in your cupboard. The odour attracts food moths which then drown in the oil. You will need at least one oil container per shelf.

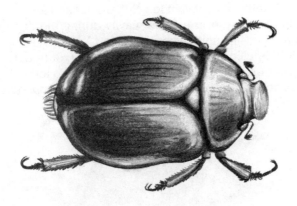

Food beetle

Last resort
If repeated cleaning of cupboards and disposal of suspect food fails to work, take all foodstuffs out of your storage area, scrub it down with soap and water and then spray with pyrethrum spray. Keep the space as sealed as possible for two or three hours, then leave the area open overnight before you replace the food.

Possums

You have only one choice with possums: you can either make friends with them or remove them. Removing them will probably mean their death: possums are very territorial and will trek for kilometres to get back home, and other possums will kill or starve them rather than let them stay in their area. A resident pair of possums will keep out strange possums – and at least you will know your residents' habits.

Well-fed possums are less inclined to go for your rose buds. So, if you choose to put up with your possums, try feeding them regularly with sweet things like apples, or even bits of stale bread, old carrots and other bits of vegetable matter in the fridge which you feel no longer tempted by. You could also try some deterrents just to keep them off new growth: spray the plants with *fresh* urine (stale urine will burn the foliage), or sprinkle on cayenne pepper or bitter alloes. A spray of diluted chilli or Tabasco sauce is excellent. You could also try netting shrubs when they have a lot of new growth.

Suburban possums mostly live in roofs – net in your eves, so they can't settle. If you want to get them out and keep them out, put a loud radio up in the roof cavity during the day – like us, possums don't like noise when they sleep. You can also spray with a horrible smelling substance like stale urine (yours, not theirs) or eucalyptus oil. If all else fails, hire a mobile disco for half an hour. The flashing lights and loud music will have your possums out of there and yelling at you within a few minutes.

Rodents – rats and mice

There are many rodent species that may become pests. Symptoms include: droppings – small, black, and curled – a characteristic, sour smell (native mice probably won't have this odour; to a limited extent it depends on what they have been eating), chewed paper, soap etc., scuttlings in corners or scamperings in the ceiling. Brown rats will also attack people, especially children. Several rat fleas will also bite people.

Rodent plagues seem to be mainly related to the availability of food. If food sources explode after a drought, so will rodent populations: to be checked as predator populations build up to match them. Rodents have a short gestation period, reach sexual maturity early, and have large litters. They can reach plague proportions in months.

Many native rodents have suffered drastic reductions in numbers since white settlement, and at least seven are now extinct. If you suspect you have native rats or mice, try to tolerate them and protect them. If possible, catch rodents in live traps first so you can identify them.

Hazards of commercial pesticides

Coumatetralyl is an anticoagulent – dangerous to pets, children and small animals like marsupial mice you may not want to kill.

Endrin is an extremely poisonous chlorinated hydrocarbon; it also kills birds.

Warfarin is another anticoagulant – very poisonous to pets and humans; rats and mice are increasingly resistant to it.

Bush rat

The common bush rat is *Rattus fuscipes*. It has dense, soft, grey-brown fur, darker on top than below, with a grey-brown or black tail, slightly shorter than the head and body. The ears are pink-grey or brown, big and round, and stick up.

The bush rat is common over most of east-coast Australia and southern Western Australia. It likes thick ground cover: heavy undergrowth anywhere, from sub-alpine areas to the coast to the fringe of rainforests. Bush rats seem to be most common in forest gullies with damp fallen logs for shelter. They seem to prefer insects but eat plant food and most other things if there is a food shortage, and will eat a bait of rolled oats and peanut butter in traps.

The bush rat reproduces throughout the year up to about five litters and may start to breed at about four months. They dig small burrows between two and three metres long, usually in rocky areas or in undergrowth, or shelter in fallen hollow logs.

You are unlikely to find bush rats inside unless you have damp forests or forest-like garden around you. We have bush rats occasionally inside as do friends in other forest areas, but if they do invade suburban homes they don't seem to have been identified as bush rats yet.

Because of colour variations, it is difficult for the amateur to tell bush rats from introduced rats at a glance. Bush rat droppings are the same colour as those of introduced rats: dark brown or black when fresh, musky smelling, and paler brown when dry. They do contain particles of insects and plant material, however, that the droppings from introduced rats probably won't have; though in similar situations the diets of both may be similar. Introduced rats are more likely to have bits of cereal in their droppings – but bush rats will also eat cereal. (Around my house they seem particularly fond of apricot kernels and will grind the seeds on rocks till they open; they also like hen food.)

Introduced rats leave bigger tracks than native rats and have bigger feet. This, of course, is not much use unless you have two to compare.

Black rat

These rats probably came with the First Fleet and have been spreading ever since, both around houses and through farmland and bush except where there is not enough water to sustain them.

The black rat is the plague rat. It likes climbing. If you have rats in your roof they are likely to be black rats: they are also known as roof rats or tree rats. The black rat eats almost anything that is living or has once lived. In forest areas it can live exclusively on underground fungi. It will predate young birds and eggs as well as carrion. It will climb fruit trees to eat the fruit, corn stalks to eat the cobs, and tables to get to left-over meals. The black rat appears to co-exist with the bush rat. We certainly have both here, each occupying their own niche.

Black rats are mostly grey-black to pale brown. The body is

slender, the tail longer than the head and body, the ears large and thin. They can have up to six litters a year of five to ten offspring and are mature at three to four months. They build large, untidy nests of shredded paper, grass or bark, preferably up high in roofs or walls or hollow trees, but also in reed beds, etc. They may also dig short burrows. In the wild they rarely live more than a year, but they can live up to three years in captivity.

Brown rat

This is *Rattus norvegicus*. It mostly lives in and around cities, but has been found in farmhouses and along wet creek banks. It prefers burrows to climbing and is mostly found around cellars and sewers and warehouses. You can usually tell a brown rat from a black rat or bush rat. Brown rats and black rats will cower and try to get away. Brown rats were probably the rats of Hameln in the fairy story. They are the dominant rats of Europe. Usually paler than black rats, they are grey-brown on top and grey to white underneath, and the fur is usually scruffier. The tail is short and thick and often scabby and the ears are short: quite different from the slender ears of the black rat and the large, round ears of the bush rat. Brown rat droppings are usually deposited in groups; black rat droppings are scattered all over the place and the ends are less pointed than brown rat droppings.

Brown rats have been domesticated and bred for colour, and more docile strains are reared as pets and for laboratories. The brown rat is also the white rat. Some people claim that keeping a white rat will keep away black rats: the black rat is scared of the brown rat odour. I haven't been able to test this. Brown rat nests are more tidy than those of black rats, and are made of paper, bark or grass, and are often under floors or in crates. They may also dig a short burrow.

Diseases spread by rats in Australia

Eosinophilic meningitis   This is spread by rat faeces to an intermediate host: a garden snail, slug, water or uncooked vegetables like lettuce.

Camphylobacter infection (Vibrosis)   Rat faeces may contaminate water along with other modes of transmission. This disease is characterised by explosive diarrhoea, headache, nausea with persistent abdominal pain for some days and other complications.

Letospirosis This is spread through infected urine of wild and domestic animals, including rats. It may be transmitted through swimming or wading in infected water. Mild cases are characterised by headache, malaise, neck stiffness, sometimes vomiting and diarrhoea lasting about nine days with frequent relapses. In severe forms there may be jaundice, nephritis, and haemorrhage.

Murine typhus The infectious faeces of rat fleas spread this disease, either through a puncture wound or through scratching. Symptoms include chills, headache, rash on the body on the fifth day, and possibly nausea.

Interstitial plasma cell pneumonia This is spread by wild and domestic animals including rats. It is usually fatal if not treated, but uncommon in Australia.

Streptobacillary rat bite fever This is spread by rat bites and general contamination, e.g. of milk contaminated by rat faeces. Symptoms include chills, fever even after the bite has healed, malaise, flare-up of the wound with relapsing fever possible for several weeks.

Spillary rat bite fever Spread by rat bites, this disease produces chills, fever even after the bite has healed, malaise, flare-up of the wound with relapsing fever possible for several weeks.

Salmonellosis Rats may spread salmonella to human and animal food through infected faeces. Make sure rats are kept out of animal food sheds. Symptoms of salmonella poisoning include headache and vomiting. Diarrhoea is usually absent or mild. It may have severe complications and can be fatal.

House mouse

The house mouse (*Mus musculus*) is probably found throughout the world. It is found all over Australia and populations can grow to plague proportions, especially in good crop years following bad ones, or about 18 months after bushfires. There have been over 20 plagues in Australia since 1960.

The house mouse is brown to black on top, paler below. Their tails are the same length or a little longer than their bodies.

A place inhabited by house mice smells 'mousy', with small piles of droppings usually pointed at both ends. They nest anywhere that seems safe: in walls, ceilings, old fence posts, trees, hen-yards, and wood heaps. The nests are made from any shredded material available.

Chestnut mouse

If you have these you will suspect at once they aren't house mice. Chestnut mice (*Psuedomys gracilaudatus* or *Psuedomys nanus*) are rounded, soft and fluffy, like a child's fur mouse. Their tails are slightly shorter than their bodies. They have slightly furry feet, with hairs that protrude over the toes, small round ears and a much blunter nose than the house mouse. They are chestnut on top, paler below.

Chestnut mice are found from woodland to heathland. They have so far been recorded along coastal New South Wales and Queensland, and in northern Western Australia and the Northern Territory. In limited areas they can be quite common.

Chestnut mice build nests of woven grass either above ground or in burrows. They like plant material and seeds though their diet will vary with availability.

New Holland mouse

This 'mouse' (*Psuedomys novaehollandia*) was once presumed extinct, but has been found to be relatively common in limited areas. So far it has been found along coastal New South Wales, southern Victoria and northern Tasmania, but may be much more widespread and simply confused with the house mouse.

New Holland mice are grey-brown on top and grey-white below. They can be easily be told from house mice by their tails – which are brown on top and white underneath – and much longer than their bodies: at least 10 to 15 per cent. I also think they are cuter and fluffier than house mice but that may be prejudice. Their noses aren't so long and 'rodent-like'.

New Holland mice build long complex tunnels, some up to five metres with nests at the bottom. They appear to breed up if any area is disturbed by fire, sand mining, or clearing. They eat almost anything, appearing to prefer seeds in spring, insects in winter, with leaves, flowers and fungi; but some I kept in captivity, for a while tried everything they were given.

Identification

Black rat Timid; likes roofs and climbing; droppings don't have the points of a brown rat and are usually deposited singly; females have 10 nipples though occasionally 11 or 12; the tail is longer than the body; the ears long and thin, usually darker and not as obviously pale underneath as the bush rat.

Brown rat Aggressive, scruffy, likes ground areas; confined mostly to cities but occasionally appears in farms and creeks; pointed droppings in groups; females have 12 nipples; tail is the same size as the body or slightly shorter; ears are short.

Bush rat Timid; tail shorter than head or body; big round ears; soft and furry; not as long and sleek as the black rat; much the same colour as the brown rat but the tail is more slender, the ears bigger, the nose blunter and the whole animal rounder, furrier and better-tempered.

You will be likely to find bush and brown rats in the same area, though bush and black rats overlap.

House mouse Tail is about the same length as body or only slightly longer; females have five pairs of nipples.

Chestnut mouse Body is usually the same size as tail or slightly shorter; small round and fluffy; slightly hairy feet.

New Holland mouse Tail brown on top, white below and at least 10 per cent longer than body.

There are many native rats and mice and rat- and mouse-like species that can be mistaken for black or brown rats or house mice. If at all in doubt, send a specimen to your local museum, CSIRO, or State Department of Agriculture for identification.

Prevention and control

Prevention is the only sure guard against rodent invasion.

Clean up all areas around the house that may provide nesting sites such as brush and long grass, especially by fences. Paved areas around the house deter rodents from crossing. Vermin-proof all food containers outside.

Make sure your house is rodent proof: that they can't get under the eaves, that windows are all screened, that doors fit well. You can buy rubber bits to stick on the bottom if they leave gaps. Rats and mice can squeeze through unbelievably tiny places. I once left a parmesan cheese container with a perforated lid on the bench.

Two days later it was empty, except for mice droppings. The openings were about the same size as apple seeds. A mouse can get through a 1 cm hole. A rat can squeeze through an opening as high as the width of your finger. Tough flyscreen is the best answer. Install metal shields on all pipes leading into the house or on to the roof. Cover any area that might be gnawed through to effect an entry with metal sheeting. Check all holes into the house. Timber floors aren't vermin proof. If you are designing a house or shed, try to have concrete floors wherever food will be kept, or use a tough floor covering, well sealed at the edges.

Owls and many other birds, including kookaburras, hawks, and other birds of prey, reptiles and foxes are all rodent predators. Open areas around houses, sheds and fences will help them catch their prey by making the rats and mice more visible. Cats and some dogs, especially terriers, will catch rodents but they will also catch rodent predators and keep birds from the garden.

Repellents

Once rodents are inside the house, fresh or dried mint leaves, lavender, white helebore or camphor or mothballs are said to repel them – and rodents are cautious of many strong odours. But no repellent will keep away a plague of rodents – at most they may keep them from your more valuable possessions like papers. Once they are inside they have to eat something, and no deterrent will keep them from a favoured foodstuff, especially if there is nothing else handy.

Traps and baits

With practice, traps are quick to set. Try lining them against a wall – at least a dozen of them for large numbers – set at right angles, with the trigger closest to the wall. Rodents often scuttle against walls, using them as sheltered runways. With large numbers of traps, don't bother about baiting them individually. Just scatter corn meal or wheat germ above them in a trail against the wall. Try and keep the wall free of other objects so the rodents can use their highway in peace. Once the traps have been used a couple of times, sprinkle them with anise oil to disguise their odour, or Chinese five spice powder, available in most supermarkets.

Other effective baits are a mixture of honey and peanut butter, bread, bacon rind around raisins, and of course cheese – though this isn't really the most preferred food and goes hard and stale faster than the other baits. I've found chocolate very tempting to

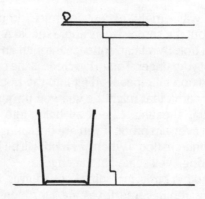

rodents, especially chocolate-coated peanuts, and it stays fresh a long time in traps in sheds awaiting the casual passing rat. If possible though, use fresh bait every day. If you have a cunning rodent that keeps taking bait, wrap a little fuse wire onto it, and tie it to the 'bait hook' or the trap. The rodent will pick up the bait and try to carry it away – and set off the trap.

A rat bait that won't kill anything else is dried potato. It is too expensive to use for large plagues, but may be useful for small problems. Leave out bowls of dried potato. The rats gorge on it and die when they take water. I've tried it twice: once effectively, once not. I suspect it depends on whether the rats have other food to tempt them away from a single massive gorge on the dried potatoes. You can also try a mixture of 1 part cement dust to 1 part icing sugar. Result: terminal constipation – and the bodies won't kill cats, dogs or birds that eat them.

If you don't want to kill your rodents (you may suspect they are native species or simply don't like killing) the following trap is easy to set up. Take a large bucket or drum, the deeper the better. Place it under a bench or table. Put a ruler on the bench, so that half of it is on the bench and half over the bucket. Now put the bait on the suspended end of the ruler. The rodents run out to the bait and fall into the bucket. This trap can also be used to drown rodents: just half-fill the bucket with water. This is a slower death than conventional traps and more cruel.

Closed traps

There are now closed traps on the market for people who dislike 'snap' traps. You just bait them and empty them. Look for advertisements in rural papers.

Silverfish

Silverfish have softer bodies than cockroaches. They are fast-scuttling, oval insects covered with soft scales, ranging from grey-white to pale silver-brown. Their bodies taper to three tail appendages. There are five species of silverfish in Australia that are a nuisance to humans. Probably all were introduced. Most native silverfish are vegetarian. One species prefers paper and glue and this is the one that is the major problem indoors. It grows to about 15 mm. Often the first symptoms of silverfish are chewed books and posters. Silverfish live for about four years and breed throughout this time. Eggs take from 10 to 60 days to hatch.

Hazards of commercial pesticides

Dichlorvos pest strips may induce asthma – never hang them in wardrobes. Dichlorvos is an organophosphate and depresses cholinesterase levels in the body, affecting the nervous system. The dichlorvos evaporates from pest strips and may affect people around it or food in cupboards. It is carcinogenic even at exposures from flea collars and pest strips. It may trigger asthmatic attacks, skin problems, convulsions. It is also associated with depression, weakness and flu-like symptoms that may be difficult to recognise. It kills birds, bees and fish.

Bendiocarb is mildly toxic. Make sure it doesn't touch your skin. Symptoms include body pains, tremors, excessive sweating, headaches and a general sense of nervousness and tension. Bendiocarb persists for several months and can poison pets, fish and birds as well as humans.

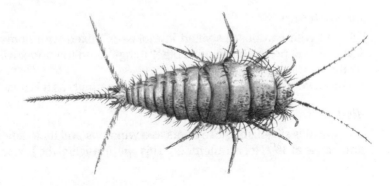

Camphor is poisonous if swallowed. Keep out of the reach of children. Even the vapour may affect a young child, though not in amounts usually found in cupboards or lingering on clothing. Use with caution.

Prevention and control

Spiders eat a large number of silverfish. A spider-infested house will have few silverfish. Encourage spiders – especially the giant huntsman spiders that don't build dust-collecting webs.

Regular vacuuming is the best prevention for silverfish. Make sure all bookcases have their contents removed at least once a year and that both books and shelves are vacuumed, as well as woody crevices in walls and other hiding places.

If books have to be left undisturbed for a long time, vacuum them or leave them out in the hot sunlight for a day, then seal them in plastic bags with lavender oil or bunches of lavender. If they have to stay in the bookcase, douse the shelves liberally with lavender oil. This will act as a deterrent for up to a year, depending on the potency of the oil and weather conditions, and how generous you were with it.

Dried or fresh bay leaves or pennyroyal oil are also reputed to keep away silverfish. Try laying bay leaves down on the shelves of your bookcase before you put in the books. A simple repellent is a liberal scatter of dried cloves along shelves.

In bad cases, or where time is limited, spray shelves with pyrethrum spray to kill the silverfish, or sprinkle borax on the shelves or behind the backing of pictures (the silverfish will lick the borax off their feet), then use lavender or bay leaves scattered along the shelves as repellents when silverfish have not been seen for several months.

Silverfish trap

Fill a lid with cardboard soaked in molasses mixed with borax. Silverfish will prefer this to most other things – and the borax will kill them.

Only a very little borax is needed – use it sparingly as it is toxic.

Heat

Dry heat kills silverfish. Close doors and windows and try to keep your house at 46°C for an afternoon. This will 'fumigate' the house.

Spiders

Spiders are perhaps a house's most valuable predator. Leave them alone if you can. Spiders eat a range of pests, including silverfish, young cockroaches, flies and mosquitoes.

Many people justify employing pest control companies because of spiders. They weigh up their family's safety with funnel-webs and red-backs against the possible, long-term and indirect consequences of spraying with residual pesticides.

Hazards of commercial pesticides

Chlorpyrifos is an organophosphate. It is less likely to be absorbed through the skin than other organophosphates, but you still need to wear protective clothing when using it. It is toxic if swallowed. Never use pressure packs containing chlorpyrifos as you may inhale the vapour.

Bendiocarb is mildly toxic. Make sure it doesn't touch your skin. Symptoms include body pains, tremors, excessive sweating, headaches and a general sense of nervousness and tension. It persists for several months and can poison pets, fish and birds as well as humans.

Funnel-web spiders

Funnel-web spiders are large, black and shiny. They rear aggressively when they are about to strike. Funnel-webs live in burrows in moist, concealed spots – under piles of rock or wood or rubbish piles. Their burrows *do not* look like funnels. Males migrate in summer looking for females. This is the time they can slip into your shoes, bed or folds of your towel. Fumigation won't stop migrating males coming inside. It may just give you a groundless sense of security.

Funnel-web bites can be fatal. Seek medical attention at once. Wash off any venom on the skin and bind the bite firmly. Keep the victim as still as possible.

Red-back spiders

Female red-backs have a distinctive red stripe. Males don't; they are harmless. Red-backs make their webs in the shade – under

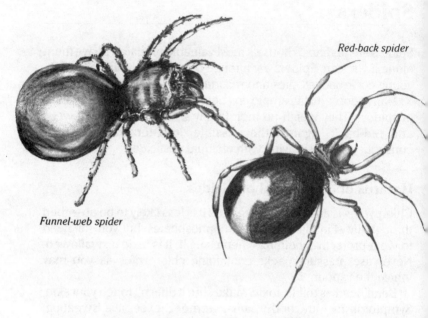

Red-back spider

Funnel-web spider

steps, in old boxes and rubbish heaps. Regular sweeping and cleaning up rubbish is the best red-back prevention – and having a healthy population of larger spiders. Black house spiders and other spiders eat red-backs.

Place ice packs on a red-back bite and get medical advice at once.

Black house spider

The black house spider builds messy webs in the corner of windows and under eaves. They are often mistaken for funnel webs. Their bite is painful, but not fatal, and they won't bite unless you provoke them. House spiders help control red-back spiders and a wide range of insects. Try to think of them as family pets. (Dogs bite too.)

Huntsman spiders

Huntsmen are the large brown to black spiders that terrify many people – without good reason. They eat many insects, from flies to moths to silverfish and small cockroaches. Their bite hurts, but isn't dangerous. They only bite if threatened.

Wolf spiders

Like funnel-webs, wolf spiders live in outdoor burrows. They may come inside after rain. They are often mistaken for funnel-web spiders. Their bites are painful, but not fatal.

White-tailed spiders

White tailed spiders have had a bad press. Their bite doesn't cause terrible recurring ulcers. They mostly eat other spiders, and sometimes silverfish. They can shelter among the bedclothes.

Note: Like any bite, spider bites can become infected, and allergic reactions are possible.

Prevention and control

Unfortunately, residual poisons don't work well with spiders. You will get rid of the initial population – and it may be some time before the population builds up again – but spiders need direct contact with insecticide for it to be effective. You will get no residual control.

It will be cheaper, less harmful and as effective to simply spray the house thoroughly with a pyrethrum insecticide yourself. Spray under all furniture, in cracks, under steps, etc. and, especially for funnel-web control, around patio plants, pot-plants and other most debris-laden places, including garden areas close to the house.

Make sure spiders aren't brought in on firewood. Use a sealed woodbox if possible or only bring in the wood that you can burn immediately. Clean up the debris round the house and wear gloves if moving any material that's been stored for a long time.

Screen doors on a spring so they close themselves, and screened windows and sealed floors are the best spider prevention. Use a sealing gun to close up cracks in floor boards, skirtings etc.

Brush down spider webs with a broom if they are annoying you. The most common poisonous spiders in Australia aren't particularly visible anyway. If the webs don't bother you but Aunt Bertha is critical, say they're the kids' science project or you are doing a survey of wildlife in the suburbs.

Powdered sulphur along shelves and in storage places is an old-fashioned spider repellent. It deters them, but doesn't kill them. Bordeaux spray (copper sulphate and lime) may also be used. My spider prevention weapons are limited to broom, dustpan and the sole of my shoe for migrating funnel-webs.

How to get a spider off the ceiling

Most 'terrifying' spiders are large 'huntsmen' on doors or ceilings. If a spider is above you and you think it is going to jump on you (it almost certainly won't) try puffing on it, or fanning it with a paper. Spiders are sensitive to air movement and even a small 'huff' may cause it to move away. Or cover it with a glass or jar – then slip a piece of paper over the rim – and let the spider out outside.

Arachnophobia

This is an unreasonable fear of spiders. Try to persuade arachnophobes to get counselling – or let them gradually become accustomed to harmless spiders if the phobia isn't severe.

Termites

Termites aren't ants in spite of their nickname 'white ants'. The main similarities are that both ants and termites are small, social, and they live in large colonies. There are at least 240 species of termite in Australia.

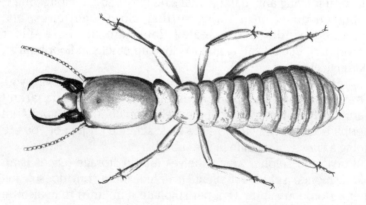

Termites eat houses. They like woody material and invade houses from their nests, often underground and often a considerable distance away, then carry food back to the nest. Termites are active, soft-bodied and white-cream to pale brown. They dislike light, preferring warmth, darkness and damp and are usually found in large numbers.

Most termites that you see will be workers: wingless and sterile, tunnelling and bringing food back to the nest. They are the termites that do the damage. The soldiers have darker heads and strong jaws but are also wingless and sterile. The other termites you may see are the winged young adults. These are produced by each colony every year. They swarm from the nest usually just after or before rain. They settle on the ground, drop their wings, mate, excavate a chamber and gradually colonies grow from these new kings and queens. Most colonies only have one king and queen. If these are destroyed the colony may die, though in some cases they may be replaced.

Wood-dwelling termites live in galleries they excavate in wood on which they feed. They don't need to keep in contact with the soil. Subterranean termites need to stay in contact with the ground to build their nests. Unfortunately it is a myth that if you destroy their tunnels to the ground you will kill them. They will be severely inconvenienced but control is unlikely.

Usually only worker termites and soldiers visit feeding sites like firewood piles. They will not be able to reproduce and form a nest, so bringing them inside with firewood is little risk, as long as the wood is burnt quickly, so termites don't get into the habit of entering the house, and as long as the wood pile is some distance away. The termites are unlikely to be able to survive long by themselves. Don't keep firewood next to the house and always move the pile at least once a year, if not every six months, in case a colony forms there and travels underground to your house.

Termites in firewood may also be dry-wood termites. These don't attack buildings.

Symptoms

There are three ways to tell if you have a termite problem:
- signs of damage in the wooden parts of your house (try prodding wooden window sills or panelling with a screwdriver);
- termite passageways over concrete piers or house footings; and

• termite nests near the house.

Termite damage in wood is unmistakable. The long tunnels just inside the wood follow the grain and never quite reach the surface. The wood may look as though it is about to collapse, or it may buckle inwards. It will also sound hollow when tapped. Termites 'plaster' up their tunnels. They also make passages roofed with this mud-like substance to travel over non-woody places where they can't chew tunnels. These passages over footings and girders are also an indication of termite infestation.

Termites enter houses from long tunnels starting at their nest. This can be a considerable distance away: often about 30 to 50 metres, sometimes more. They return to the nest with food. Different kinds of termites build different nests. These are usually mounds, in hollow trees or underground. They also like warmth and moisture, and often build their nests near underground pipes. If you find a termite nest near your house, the termites must be feeding somewhere. It is safest to destroy the nest.

Don't mistake termite damage for beetle larvae damage or fungal rot. Fungal attack leaves the wood soft, sometimes darker, and brittle, sometimes dampish to touch. There are no passages or chambers. The larvae of wood-boring beetles make sawdust filled tunnels and leave by small holes – about 2 to 3 mm. Sawdust deposits probably mean borers, not termites (see 'Wood borers').

Hazards of commercial pesticides

Termite control is possibly Australia's largest pesticide polluter, with the widest consequences for human and environmental health. Yet, because many of these side-effects are hidden or long-term, and because we have an almost superstitious fear of the damage termites can do, most people prefer to shut their eyes to the consequences and leave the matter in the hands of a pest control company.

Poisons to control termites should not be necessary if a house is designed to minimise vulnerability to termites and if the structural wood is regularly examined (see 'Prevention and control', below). Even when termites invade a house, there are still several options to be tried before resorting to spraying.

Most termite control has relied on strong and persistent chemicals because termites can go unnoticed till major structural damage has occurred. Most builders routinely arrange for spraying before foundations are laid.

Until 1953 the main control was blowing arsenic trioxide dust into the cavities of infected wood. The termites brushed against this and carried it back to the nest. Arsenic is extremely poisonous, and is usually only effective when used by an experienced person who knows the habits of the different termite species. If you intend to get a pest controller in, ask them to identify the termites. If they can't, call another firm.

Nowadays, most houses have a chemical soil barrier. This is usually one of the organochloride insecticides such as chlordane, heptachlor, dieldrin or aldrin. These are effective for 30-50 years. An organophosphorous chlorpyrifos is also becoming more popular. It is effective for about five years.

These chemical barriers only protect the ground around the house – they don't kill termite colonies.

No reputable pest controller should pressure you into annual sprayings of organophosphorous or organochloride treatments.

None of the organochlorides used for termite control in Australia can be used in the USA, because of their probable effects on human health and the environmental damage they would cause. Organochloride spraying has been associated with short-term problems like irritability, lethargy, nausea, asthma, headaches in children, miscarriage, and susceptibility to viruses in the month following spraying. In the longer term, spraying has been associated with muscle weakness and nervous system problems. Organochlorides bio-accumulate in the food chain, and high levels are found in breast milk. They have also been associated with birth defects and miscarriages.

Aldrin has been associated with liver cancer in mice. Lindane has been associated with pernicious aenemia and leukemia. Chlordane has been found to be carcinogenic in animals; it is stored in fatty tissue and can be released after stress or dieting. Heptachlor has been associated with miscarriage and birth deformities. Organophosphates have been implicated in birth defects, asthma, and allergic reactions, and long-term muscle weakness or pins and needles.

All these sprays kill all insect life, as well as fish and earthworms. Birds eat the affected insects and are killed too.

Arsenic is poisonous and may be carcinogenic; however, residues are removed by the pest controller after the termites are killed. This technique is probably far safer than the two conventional alternatives, but the operator must be skilled in pest control – not just in using pesticides.

Prevention and control

There are two ways to control termite damage: prevent them entering the house at all, and destroy the nests. Both must be used for effective control. Most termite control has relied on strong and persistent chemicals because termites can go unnoticed till major structural damage has occurred. Most builders routinely arrange for spraying before foundations are laid. This is not necessary if the house is designed to minimise vulnerability to termites, and if the structural wood is regularly examined.

No organic termite control will be effective unless either the nest has been destroyed or the house has been made 'termite proof' so that you can see if they are re-entering. No organic control is 'persistent': it simply gives you a breathing space to get to the root of the problem.

In several major cities there are organic pest control agents listed in the telephone book. With termites it pays to get an expert in, if only because they will be experienced at diagnosing the extent of the problem. If there are none in your city, at least try to talk to an interstate company by phone. Don't just depend on any pest control company you pick out of the phone book. Many rely on the strength and persistence of their chemicals alone and know very little about the ecology of the pests they are eradicating. As a general guide, ask any pest control agent what species of termite you have, and what their habits are. If they don't know, find an agency that does know termites.

Before you build

Consider stone, steel framing, pise (rammed earth), brick, concrete or mud brick, etc. in termite-prone areas.

Always use ant-capping or steel posts. Ant-capping forces termites to build their tunnels over the capping, where they can be easily seen and removed. Ant-capping does not keep termites out of the house, but it does make them visible so you can destroy the nest in the area. The capping may also slow them down so that there is less damage by the time you recognise the infestation. Ant-capping must be checked every three to six months. Make sure capping is also placed over hollows in double-brick walls which may become termite corridors leading to roof timber.

Seal all cracks and joins in concrete, stone, or earthen construction to stop termite access to the house. Consider a protruding metal 'ridge' about 100 mm up in earth walls, so that termites must build out around it where you can see them.

If your building is to have a suspended floor, make sure the ground below will be well-drained and ventilated: dampness encourages termites. Make sure that you can get under the floor easily to check for termites at least every six months. Leave a gap of at least half a metre, if not more. Some termites (*Coptotermes frenchi*) are able to build free-standing galleries from soil to the floor above.

Make the area as unattractive to termites as possible. Clear away dead wood and roots of trees. Make very sure that all building debris is cleared away as soon as possible. Check any trees near the house to see if they are termite infested.

Consider termite-resistant wood like river red gum, jam acacia or American redwood. Ask your local Department of Agriculture office for local woods that are resistant to local termite species.

CSIRO is testing the effectiveness of layers of ground basalt and granite under slabs and suspended floors. Termites appear to avoid ground basalt as it's hard to move through. CSIRO is also researching a gut nematode parasite to control termites. 'Termaguard' ground granite barriers are commercially available. These can be used under or around your foundations or as deep trenches or 'moats' around the house. 'Termaguard' has proved very effective overseas, and in some areas of Australia, but at the time of writing has to been tested in the long term with all Australian termite species, or under all climate conditions.

After building

Check under the floor at least every six months for termite galleries. Check capping, footings, etc. regularly for passageways.

Scrutinise any old wooden furniture or firewood you bring into the house. If there is termite damage or it feels light and rotten, don't bring it inside.

Don't keep firewood piled up next to the house for long periods. Only bring in as much wood as you need to burn for a few hours.

Make termite traps. Drive rough-sawn hardwood stakes, about 30 cm long and 5 cm square, into the soil around your house: near old trees, and along garden beds. Pound the stakes well into the soil till only the tops show. Take them out every six months or so and check for termite damage. If it's there, the chances are your house may be infested too. The more 'traps' you have, the easier it will be to trace the termite nest: the nearer stakes will probably be damaged first.

A more complex but effective device has been developed by Dr John French and Dr Bob Rich. In a slightly adapted form, this involves surrounding your house with narrow polythene pipe, just under soil level. Now take six old ice-cream containers; punch holes in lid and base, and fill with damp corrugated cardboard. Cut the pipe, attach it to the containers, and check them every month. If the cardboard has been eaten you have termites.

Eradicating termites

Take a sample of the termites. Preserve them in methylated spirits diluted with one-third water. If you can't identify them yourself from the notes here, take them to a pest control company if there is a reliable one in your city, to the CSIRO, the Department of Agriculture or Forestry, or a natural history museum. Once you know what sort of termite you have, you will know what sort of nest to look for.

Destroy the nest. This is the most important step and must be taken at once. Once the nest is destroyed the infestation will stop. Some workers may be able to survive for a year or two but these can easily be killed with a pyrethrum spray.

Once the nest is destroyed, remove all infested wood. Follow the tunnels to see where the termite influence extends. Use a strong pyrethrum solution all around the infested area. Check frequently. Remember: the pyrethrum will kill the termites feeding in the house but will not kill those in the nest. Until the nest has been destroyed they will keep re-infesting your house.

Install barriers in your house so that a further infestation won't go unnoticed.

Don't panic. Termites move relatively slowly and won't gobble your house up in the few days it takes to locate their nest. Don't tear out all damaged wood. It may still be structurally useful, and the termites will just move elsewhere anyway.

Destroying nests

Mounds   These are easily noticed. They are unlike to be more than 30 metres away from the house (though other termites nests may be much further away), may be in a bushy corner of the garden or under the house. Dig the mound up. It shouldn't extend far underground. The 'nursery' will be near the centre of the mound. Break up the mound once it is dug and up and spray thoroughly with a pyrethrum spray. If you don't want to use any spray at all, submerge the lot in water for at least three weeks.

Make sure the termites can't escape.

Nests in trees   These may not be obvious. Look for broken branches and hollows in the tree: the sort of hollows that possums or parrots nest in. Then drill the tree to see if it is hollow. All trees over 40 cm wide and within 50 to 60 metres of the house should be checked for termites if your house is infected. Use an auger bit 12 to 19 mm in diameter, boring downwards slightly towards the centre of the tree. Drill at least twice, once near the roots and again about a metre up. If there are termites, the auger will suddenly shoot into the tree as it reaches the muddy tunnel filling.

If you find a hollow but are not sure if there are termites there, stick a bit of dowel into the hole, wait two weeks, pull it out and see if it is damaged, chewed or spotted brown with droppings, or if a few termites come out with it.

The safest thing to do now is to burn the tree. If you don't want to eradicate the tree as well as the termites, (and this would be my preferred option) climb as far up the tree as you can, drill fairly wide holes and funnel in strong pyrethrum spray. Check the nest with dowel and auger three days later. If there are still live termites, repeat the procedure until none remain, and check the tree at monthly intervals for at least a year to make sure there is no renewed activity. If you treat the trees in autumn and the termites appear to vanish, always check the trees again in spring in case their disappearance was only seasonal.

Underground nests   These are more difficult to detect. Look for places where roots appear to be dying back, indicating root damage below, and for bare patches or dying tops of trees and shrubs. Some underground nests are formed like mounds below the soil; others are long passageways. Sometimes the termite traps mentioned above are the only way of distinguishing these nests. Use the controls suggested for 'ants': kerosene emulsion, pyrethrum, etc. These may have to repeated several times to make sure all passageways have been cleared. Nests may also be dug up, but be careful that long passageways have not been missed. Be careful and thorough. Termites may seal off damaged parts of their colony.

Hardy termites   If you fail to find the termite nests, or if infestation continues, a non-organic but last resort is arsenical dusting. Small quantities of dust are blown into the galleries where the termites are feeding. The arsenic is then taken back to their nests, which are poisoned as dead termites are eaten by the living. The whole nest is poisoned over several days. After you have dusted, the damaged areas should be sealed. Don't try arsenical dusting yourself. Contact a pest control company and tell them explicitly what you want done; then leave it to them. Don't be talked into preventive spraying. If you are vigilant and aware that termites may invade again, there is no need to take any action till the pests actually appear.

Arsenic traps   If you don't want arsenic in your house, fill a fruit box with old wood and arsenic; bury it near the nest or next to the damaged part of your house. The termites will carry the arsenic back to their colony, killing it.

Keeping up prevention

- Be wary of plants against walls if termites can tunnel up under their cover.
- Make sure steps, pergolas, etc. have ant-caps too.
- Don't store boxes, wood, etc. under the house where they may attract termites or help them to get up to a suspended floor.
- Regular inspection is the only way to keep a house free of termites.

Wasps

If you need to clear wasps' nests from your house, knock them down either at night or in winter when they are dormant, burn the residue, and spray with pyrethrum spray at night, or with a strong-smelling deterrent like eucalyptus oil or tea tree oil if there is any further interest in the area. Try to identify the sort of wasp first. If they are European wasps, get rid of them fast. If they aren't European wasps and don't appear to be interested in you, try to tolerate them.

I have a large wasps' nest above the kitchen window. It doubles in size every year and when it looks as though the next doubling will take up too much window space, I knock it down. But the wasps clear up an enormous range of funnel-web and other spiders, pear and cherry slugs, cabbage-white butterfly caterpillars, and many other pests. These are paper wasps, and despite frequent provocation like washing nappies underneath

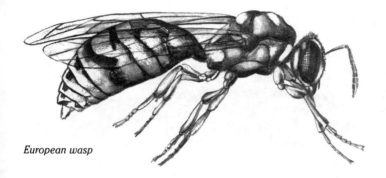

European wasp

them and putting up an exterior telephone bell just above their nest, they have not yet stung anyone.

There are mud wasps in the toilet too, that eat the spiders that eat the flies (the bats and swallows eat the bathroom flies as well) and they too haven't stung anyone yet. A ground-dwelling wasp did sting me a couple of years ago, but that was because I sat on it. It felt like a severe mosquito bite. I hope the wasp survived to eat more caterpillars from the cabbages some other day.

For a wasp in the house, use a flyswat if you can't coax it out the window and you are worried by it. Wasps can sting, but you can move faster. With the exception of the European wasp, I have never found wasps aggressive. If you have European wasps around, remember they are attracted by sweet things. Be careful, especially of opened drink cans they could be foraging in, and, of concealed nests where children might play. If you discover a nest, call the Department of Agriculture for advice.

Apart from European wasps, please ignore wasps. They are too valuable to be destroyed.

Wood borers

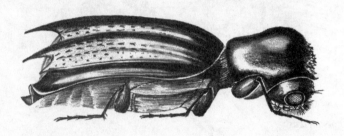

These are beetle larvae, and should not be confused with termites. Termites fill their passages with plaster-like mud and produce mud passageways. Borers fill their tunnels with sawdust, and spilled sawdust on the floor and small holes in the wood are usually the first sign of borer damage. Unfortunately these holes are made as the beetle leaves the wood, spilling out sawdust, and the damage may already have been done.

To prevent borers infesting wood in the first place, paint wood with a half borax, half methylated spirits mixture. If you do find borers in the structural wood of your house, you have a serious problem. Contact a builder first, if you are not familiar with the structure of your house, to make sure that timber doesn't have to be replaced. If it does, consider borer-resistant woods like western red cedar, redwood, white cypress pine or mountain ash, or alternative materials like stone, pisé (rammed earth), mud brick, concrete or steel. Some borers only infect sapwood, not heartwood and an infestation can be lived with.

Pyrethrum will kill wood borers but the application needs to be thorough and is not a job for the inexperienced. Lyctus borers, the main pest of structural wood, move quickly and delay may mean serious damage. Try ringing pest control companies till you find one willing to do the job with a pyrethrum-based product.

CHAPTER 2

Plants, Pets and People

Indoor plants

Most problems with indoor plants aren't from pests: they are the result of too much or too little light, under- or overfeeding, watering, fluctuations in temperature, wrong humidity and generally inappropriate conditions for that plant. There are few pests inside to worry your plants; on the other hand, those that do invade rarely have any natural predators to control them.

The best pest control for pot-plants is to wipe them over with a soapy Wettex or to remove pests by hand. Try leaving your pots outside, in broken light and a sheltered place – under a tree or on the verandah – for a few weeks. Let the predators outdoors deal with the problem, whilst sunlight, rain and natural ventilation will improve the health of your plant. If you do place your pots outside, dig them into the ground temporarily, pot and all. This will protect the roots against fluctuating temperatures and stop the pot drying out fast. Remember that the roots of potted plants are more exposed in their thin pots than those of garden plants. The smaller the pot the greater the risk of exposure.

Symptoms of poor conditions

Spots on foliage   This may be due to water marks: try not to water foliage. If dusty, wipe with a damp Wettex. Use only room-temperature water, not cold water from the tap.

Failure to flower   This is often due to insufficient water, light or uneven watering.

Leaf drop   This can be caused by insufficient water, light or uneven watering.

Foliage rolling upwards   This happens naturally in some plants, especially at night or with insufficient light; it can also be caused by draughts.

Brown leaf tips   This is probably due to dry soil or dry atmosphere. Try to improve humidity. Make sure the water you use isn't salty or high in chlorine or fluoride.

Water marks   These are pale-coloured rings, streaks or patches. Use only room-temperature water, not cold water from a tap. Try to keep water off the leaves.

White encrustation on the soil around the plant   This is due to salt build-up. Pots need frequent watering and there is nowhere for the salts – found in all Australian water supplies – to leach to. Soak the pot in fresh water for a couple of hours or re-pot with fresh mixture. Salt-affected plants may have smaller leaves, root damage or browned edges.

Causes of plant problems

Insufficient light   Plants show this in various ways: failure to flower, a strong tendency to lean towards the light; thin, untidy growth; foliage is yellowish or faded.

Too much light   House plants with too much light are often stumpy, with a clumped-together look; leaves may yellow and fall.

Old age   It's normal for many plants to have dead or dying leaves around the edges: they are simply making way for new leaves, and unlike outdoor plants there are no winds or animals in your house to remove them.

Dust   Plants need to breathe. Keep their leaves free of dust, preferably by wiping every month with a wet cloth.

Water stress   If pot-plants have dried out, they may shrink from the edges of the pot, so that when you water them the water just runs down and out without wetting the soil. These pots should be soaked in the sink or a bucket of water to swell the soil again. Try not to let them get fully dried out again.

Need for re-potting   Plants need re-potting if they start to bulb out above the pot or if the roots start curling round and round the pot. Some plants like African violets flower better when slightly pot-bound. Most flower less.

Plant tonic

If your plants are continually pest prone, they probably need a tonic, like any cold-prone child whose general health needs bolstering to increase their disease resistance.

Take a handful of as many of the following as possible:
comfrey, nettles, wormwood, chamomile flowers, yarrow, fresh green lucerne.

Use all, if possible, but any are better than no tonic at all. Cover with water in a bucket with a lid. Seal and leave for three weeks. Take off a cupful of water, dilute to the colour of weak tea and spray on the plant thoroughly, letting the residue drip into the pot. Add some more water to the bucket and put the lid on. This supply of tonic should be good until the water removed is no longer coloured. At that stage, use any residue as mulch around the pot.

Apply the tonic twice in the first week, then once a week indefinitely.

Indoor plant pests

Recipes for most of the pesticides and repellents referred to can be found in Chapter 3.

Aphids

Symptoms   There will be small insects densely clustered mostly on new growth. They can be greenish to yellowish, more rarely black-brown or reddish; leaves and sometimes flowers are distorted. Aphids insert their slender mouth parts below the surface cells of leaves, stems and buds and suck the sap. The wound is not severe but the loss of sap and injected toxins can be. Aphids may also coat the plant with honeydew which encourages sooty mould.

Solution   Place pots outside for a few weeks for predators to clear up problems. Severa – the larvae of species of lacewings – and ladybirds can eat 200 to 600 aphids. Wipe leaves with a soapy Wettex; spray with a seaweed and nettle spray; try garlic, lantana, onion or elder spray.

Caterpillars

Symptoms   Holes in the foliage.

Solution   Dipel; pick them off by hand; white-pepper spray.

Gnats

Symptoms   These are associated with decaying organic matter. They may hover over pot-plants and occasionally damage soft new growth or seedlings. Many only eat fungus.

Solution   Keep undecomposed organic matter out of your pots. If gnats are a persistent problem, try re-potting. Don't over-water plants or let them stand with wet feet. If re-potting fails to control the problem, get rid of gnat larvae (about 5 mm long, white with black heads) from the pots by standing them in pyrethrum spray for ten minutes. Do not do this without re-potting, however.

Pyrethrum breaks down quickly, and if there is still un-decomposed organic matter in your pot it may become re-infected.

Leaf eelworm

Symptoms Wedge-shaped brown or black areas on leaves, usually followed by shrivelling.

Solution Drench the pot with a one-in-ten molasses and water solution to dehydrate eelworm; keep up levels of organic matter in pot; mulch with compost or re-pot in good well-rotted compost.

Leaf hoppers (Jassids)

Symptoms Mottled fronds, especially on tree ferns.

Solution Wipe with a soapy Wettex; use garlic spray.

Mealy bugs

Symptoms Downy white patches appear on foliage or stems; may be followed by sooty mould. Mealy bugs move if you prod them. They are usually clustered together along twigs or stems or in the axils of stems and twigs. The adults are about 2 to 7 mm long with a puffy wax coat. The immature ones resemble the adults but aren't so fluffy. Plants may wilt and die, foliage may turn yellow, droop and fall off. Mealy bugs may be transported onto the plant by ants, which feed on their sweet secretions.

Solution Control ants with grease bands at the base of the plant; prune off affected foliage; place pots outside if possible for a few weeks; wipe leaves on top and bottom with a soapy Wettex or a Wettex dipped in oil; spray in cool weather.

Mites (red spider, cyclamen and African violet mite)

Symptoms The foliage will be distorted and thickened. It may be dull and pitted, sometimes with a skeletonised tracer over it. On cyclamens and African violets, purplish depressions may appear on leaves crisscrossed by fine cracks. Unfolding leaves or flowers may be distorted. Mites aren't visible with the naked eye. They reach only 1.5 mm when mature.

Solution Milk spray; wipe leaves with a soapy Wettex.

Mushroom fly

Symptoms Many tiny black insects hovering round plant.

Solution   These may be due to using mushroom compost in the potting mix. Spray plant with pyrethrum spray; soak the pot if possible in a one-in-ten water pyrethrum mix for a day.

Stag horn beetle

Symptoms   Small brown indentations in leaves; larvae tunnels and shrivelled fronds.

Solution   Spray back of leaves and centre of plant thoroughly with bug juice or garlic, quassia, wormwood or rhubarb-leaf spray.

Whitefly

Symptoms   Many tiny white flies clustered round plant; may be mottled. If you jostle a whitefly-infested plant, they should swarm up. Immature whiteflies are tiny oval greenish discs, less that 1 mm long. They stay still on the underside of leaves. Whitefly can excrete honeydew that stimulates sooty mould.

Solution   Whitefly is worse when soil is deficient in phosphorous or magnesium. Add dolomite, ground rock phosphate or wood ash to the soil. Rhubarb in easily moved pots is said to help deter whitefly from greenhouses. Wipe foliage with a soapy Wettex.

Diseases of indoor plants

Honeydew and sooty mould

Honeydew is produced by scales, aphids, mealy bugs and whiteflies. These continuously suck sap from their host plants, then excrete most of it as a heavy sugary solution. Sap suckers are voracious. Sap is low in protein and they have to suck continuously to get enough. This means a lot of fluid is excreted.

Sooty mould is a fungus that frequently grows on heavy deposits of honeydew. It can be wiped off house plants with a soapy Wettex; but that will only get rid of the sooty mould, not the problem that caused it. If you see sooty mould or a shiny sticky coating on leaves, look for the source of the problem. Of course, a very thorough wiping may get rid of the pests too. Ants like honeydew. Various ants are associated with various honeydew producers, carrying them to the source of supply and feasting on the residue. If aphids suddenly appear in your house, the chances are that they have been brought there by ants.

Ants are easily controlled around pots without resorting to insecticides.

- Place the pot in a saucer of oil.
- Place the legs of the table that the pots are on in a saucer of oil or water. This will evaporate though, and so will need topping up.
- Warm some tree-banding grease, then place a band around the pot with a broad brush or stick, or band the stem of the plant and main branches.

Scale

Symptoms   Small encrustations on leaves or stems; these may be black, green, red or brown, flat, raised or pin-sized.

Solution   Crush scale between your fingers; wipe leaves with a soapy Wettex or leave outside for a couple of weeks to let the predators get at them.

Powdery and downy mildew

Symptoms   Powdery or greyish film over foliage.

Solution   Pick off affected foliage as soon as symptoms appear; spray or wipe the remaining leaves with chive or chamomile tea, milk spray, lilac or garlic spray. Try to reduce the humidity around your plant. Remove it from hot, wet areas like the kitchen or away from other plants that need frequent watering. Never let a mildew-prone plant sit in a saucer of water or next to any other plant in a saucer of water.

Palm problems

Brown tips are caused by dry air: improve the humidity. Large brown patches often occur if plants are placed near heaters or sudden sunlight after shade. Move them. Irregular blotches on leaf margins are caused by root damage, overfeeding or wet soil. To correct overfeeding, soak the pot in water for an hour, then allow to dry out naturally. Dull leaves may be caused by root damage or possibly over-dry soil.

Pets

Pets can be host to many parasites and pests that also attack humans. Some stay on for only a few hours, some may carry disease, some – like dog fleas – may make life miserable for the whole household. Animals can also be a major cause of pests entering a house; carrying ticks, fleas or mites for example. Unhygienic eating and sleeping areas can attract flies and mosquitoes.

Pets leave detritus – hair, flakes of skin, etc. – around the pests to breed in. This means more vacuuming, and more airing of rugs and blankets is needed to stop pest outbreaks. Long-haired pets of course produce (and lose) more hair than short-haired varieties.

Make sure that pets' sleeping areas – whether they sleep on their own blanket or on your bed – are kept dry, regularly aired in the sunlight, and washed or dry-cleaned frequently.

Loose covers on chairs or sofas that can be dry-cleaned, washed or left in the sunlight are a good idea if you have pets, as are mats instead of wall-to-wall carpets. Mats can be taken outside and left in the sunlight or strongly beaten to remove pests or their eggs.

Brush or comb hairy pets often to remove loose hair, fleas, etc. Use a fine-toothed comb. Pets kept in confined areas seem more pest prone, as, possibly, are pets whose diet is deficient in vitamins.

Make sure water bowls are regularly cleaned and emptied to eradicate mosquito larvae. Wash dog dishes frequently to avoid a crusty build-up that can attract flies. Clean up faeces in confined areas. Remember it is the smell and moisture that will attract flies. Even after the faeces have been removed, moist soil underneath may still smell. If pets have to be confined for a time, concrete is better than bare soil.

Remember that domestic animals have lived with humans for a long time; and so humans and their pets have a good range of disease pests and parasites in common.

Fleas

Many fleas are capable of living on more than one host, either for long or short periods. Most people acquire dog fleas from the environment, rather than directly from their pet dog; but the dog will have been the original source none the less. People coming to an empty house that once had a pet dog or cat may be viciously attacked by starving fleas; the vibrations in the house from human movement may be enough to stimulate adult fleas to emerge from their pupae.

Human fleas will spread to animals but won't stay on them. The poultry stickfast flea will spread to humans, as will fleas from rats, cats, dogs, possums, chickens and rabbits.

Dog fleas can cause hypersensitivity in dogs. Once they start to scratch and bite they may set up a secondary infection or severe dermatitis out of all proportion to the flea infestation. 'Summer eczema' is usually caused by fleas, as the dog bites and scratches the irritated area and further flea bites aggravate previous bites. If dogs are sensitive to fleas, extreme care must be taken to keep them free of them; even a few fleas can cause eczema.

Dipylidiasis is the common dog or cat tapeworm that can be passed on to humans through accidentally swallowing dog fleas infected with the larvae. Symptoms include diarrhoea, abdominal pain and irritability. Human and cat fleas can also pass on the tapeworm.

Control

See page 27 for side-effects of commercial products.

Every dog or cat probably has about 40 000 fleas – either live ones or eggs or larvae. If you don't get rid of the eggs as well as the fleas, you'll soon have more fleas.

All fleas breed in the dust and detritus where animals sleep or lie about. No flea control will work unless it is aimed at these areas just as much as at the animal itself. Don't just check bedding. Look for 'dog nests' under the house or in a grassy spot by the fence, and remember that animals sleep on sofas and doormats – especially in their owners' absence. Once you have killed the fleas in residence, you should be able to rely on hygiene and repellents to keep areas flea-free. Remember that fleas can live for weeks or months without feeding: simply excluding pets from an area for a while won't clear up the flea problem.

Both pyrethrum and derris are very effective flea killers. Neither has much residual action, and both must be combined with treatment of sleeping areas. Use a pyrethrum wash carefully, as some people are allergic to it.

Wash animals thoroughly. Try combing through equal parts of eucalyptus oil and ammonia. Pay particular attention to the areas around the ears, neck, tail, backbone and under the legs. Alternatively, simply sponge the worst-affected areas with a Wettex dipped in home-made pyrethrum spray or equal parts of methylated spirits and water.

Derris and eucalyptus lotion is also effective for fleas, as is garlic elder lotion. Use both with care as they are poisonous, even if not long-lasting.

Leave animal bedding outside in the hot sun for several days; the eggs will die and the fleas will jump off. If there is any danger that the departing fleas might re-infest your pet, spray the bedding with a pyrethrum-based insecticide as soon as you put it outside, or soak in pyrethrum spray for half an hour, or in soapy water with derris added at the rate of one ounce to a gallon of water.

Make your own flea powder by mixing 1 part talcum powder with 2 parts crushed pyrethrum flowers, or 4 parts feverfew flowers, though the latter are not as effective. One part powdered sassafras or powdered fennel can be added to this.

There are now several good 'organic' flea powders on the market.

Derris flea powder   Derris dust can be used as a convenient flea powder. Dust straight derris powder through the animal's hair, leave it for half an hour, then brush it out. Sweep up dead or stupified fleas and burn them. Derris can also be used as a wash. Add an ounce of derris to a gallon of warm soapy water and wash the animal thoroughly.

Repellents

Repellents help to avoid further infestations. They won't kill fleas, nor will they work if you have a large hungry population of fleas with nothing else to feed on.

There is an old saying, 'Plant fennel round the kennel'. Fennel is reputed to keep away fleas. Pennyroyal oil or ointment can be combed through animals' hair, or try spreading pets' beds with stinking roger or native peppermint.

Boil up stinking roger to make a flea-repellent bath: equal parts flowers and water, strain and rinse through the animal's hair.

Wormwood or southernwood tea is another flea-repellent animal wash. Take a handful of the herb and bring to the boil in a litre of water. Let it steep till cool. Strain and use undiluted. As well as repelling, these will also kill fleas, though not as effectively as derris and pyrethrum.

Tansy, tea tree or lavender oil on bedding will also help to repel fleas. A bed of dried rue will help keep fleas from dogs; but don't use it for cats as they usually hate it. Sprinkle pennyroyal oil on pets' beds, comb it through their hair or scatter the crushed leaves where they sleep.

Fleas are also repelled by cedar wood shavings. Use them as bedding if you can get hold of them.

A teaspoon full of powdered sulphur once a week in their food is reputed to keep fleas from dogs and cats. One teaspoon is sufficient for an adult cat: the dose should be increased or decreased according to weight.

Fennel Vinegar The fennel repels fleas; the vinegar soothes eczema which can attract more fleas. Chop fennel tops; fill a jar and cover with vinegar; leave between one and three days in the sun. Dab on tail, neck and armpit areas.

Flies

Flies are attracted to odour. If your animal smells, see to its general health: its diet, whether there is eczema, infection from scratching fleas, overactive scent glands, etc. If there is no obvious cause, take it to the vet. See that bedding is frequently changed or washed and well-aired in sunlight. Dogs should be allowed to range so that their droppings aren't deposited in the same area. Get a doggie scoop and bury them, don't compost them: humans and dogs share too many diseases. Make sure blood-stained or encrusted food dishes aren't attracting flies.

Repellents

Eucalyptus oil combed through fur will keep flies from animals. I used this once on a severely injured kangaroo when no commercial preparation was effective. For large applications, add a teaspoonful of eucalyptus oil to a cup of hot water and comb through hair or fleece.

Plant a walnut tree over the kennel. This does work. I have 17 mature walnuts and many species of animal seek out the grove in summer, to rest or give birth or if they are injured. It is always free of flies. But the leaves must accumulate for some years to be effective.

If animals are flyblown, flush out the maggots with methylated spirits. This will also kill them. Brush eucalyptus oil around fur to keep flies away; but make sure it doesn't touch the wound itself.

Lice

Lice are host specific. Animal and bird lice won't persist on humans for more than a few hours, though they can be an irritation for a short time. Wash animals with a mixture of derris dust combined with two tablespoons of eucalyptus oil. Alternatively, cut the animal's hair and then wipe the skin with liquid derris mixed with eucalyptus oil. Wormwood tea should repel lice, but won't kill them.

An old Gypsy remedy for lice is to take broom twigs, crush them and just cover them with oil. Bring to the boil and steep overnight. Brush the liquid through the animal's hair. I haven't tried this and can't vouch for its effectiveness. Another old remedy I haven't tried, involves bringing two handfuls of walnut leaves or a handful of green nut cases to the boil in a litre of water. Let steep till cool and then comb through the hair or fleece.

Lice on hens

Poultry lice will cause irritability and possible damage to skin and feathers as the hens try to scratch away the irritation. Hens may be too restless to nest properly and may be more susceptible to other diseases. Lice multiply mostly in cold weather. As the entire life of a louse is spent on the host, lice control on the hen is all that is necessary: you don't have to clean up nesting areas as well. Make sure, however, that all birds are treated, and that roosting areas are netted off from wild birds.

Take either derris dust or well-pulverised pyrethrum. Mix with an equal quantity of flour or talcum powder. Place in a jar with holes pierced in the lid, or use a flour-sifter. Get a friend to hold the birds upside down. Shake the powder over the birds, making sure it penetrates well between all the feathers. Repeat two weeks later or if symptoms return.

Paint perches with a mixture of 1 part eucalyptus oil and 1 part derris dust or borax, and 1 part methylated spirits.

Mange

This is common throughout Australia, though animals with mange from Demodex mites do not always show symptoms. Good diet seems a prevention: make sure their food is rich in vitamins A and B, and high in protein.

Clip off the hair, then bathe the animal thoroughly with warm soapy water to which a little olive oil has been added. This is necessary for good penetration as the mites are deep in the skin and sebaceous glands. Then comb through derris and eucalyptus lotion.

Mites

Most mites are too small to be seen with the naked eye. Some mites may be spread from birds (including hens, starlings, etc.) and rats to people. The house mite is common on starlings and other birds and when roofs are infested the mites can spread to people and are called 'starling lice'. Mites can cause dermatitis or a rash resembling a series of flea bites. Some people show greater sensitivity than others to mite attack. Seal around your roof with chicken wire to keep birds and rats out.

Most mites can be washed off with very hot soapy water. Soak in a hot bath with a dessertspoonful of eucalyptus oil and a dessertspoonful of lavender oil added. Scrub yourself with a bristly brush, then take a long hot shower straight after your bath. A good permethrin commercial lotion is available.

Air carpets, mats, cushions, and sofa covers in the sunlight for several days or in a plastic bag outside, or have them dry-cleaned. See 'Fleas' and 'Lice' in Chapter 1 for general preventive and control measures.

If mites don't respond to soap and water or spring-cleaning, seek medical advice to determine exactly what sort of mite infestation you have. Dermatitis may remain after mites have been cleared up. If this occurs, seek medical advice.

Mites in living areas can be controlled with a thorough pyrethrum spray. Seal the room as well as possible first, and go outside for two hours afterwards. Commercial 'permethrin bombs' are available and very effective.

Commercial hazards

Some tests have shown Dicofol to be mutagenic. See 'Nits' and 'Lice'.

Scaly leg

This is caused by a minute parasite. Scrub chooks' legs with equal quantities of crushed garlic, cayenne pepper and vinegar. A preliminary wash in very soapy water will help this penetrate.

Another remedy involves washing with warm soapy water to which a little ammonia has been added. Then rub in a mixture of half garlic spray and half undiluted vinegar with a pinch of cayenne pepper, or 1 part derris dust mixed with 1 part eucalyptus oil.

Ticks

Humans can become affected by the ticks normally found on a wide variety of domestic and native animals. The common dog tick has been known to become attached to humans as well as cats, dogs and especially bandicoots and echnidnas.

The main dog tick is *Ixoides holocylus*, also known as the paralysis tick or sometimes the scrub tick. It's not indigenous to Australia and is also found in New Guinea, India and Indonesia. In Australia it is usually found within a few miles of the eastern coast but does extend inland along valleys and waterways. It has been found, but is not common, in Western Australia. Its range is increasing.

The dog tick needs humid conditions to thrive. Ticks die if the temperature drops to 7°C for a few days.

It is the female tick that attaches and sucks blood, though male ticks may be found among hair. Eggs hatch in 49 to 61 days, and the larvae harden and attach to a host about a week later. After feeding for four to six days they drop off, moult, and after anywhere from 19 to 41 days they attach again for another four to seven days, engorge and drop off again. Three to ten weeks later their development is complete and they attach again to a host. The female engorges from one to three weeks, then drops to the ground to lay two to three thousand eggs. The colder the weather the longer the tick appears to feed.

Ticks are active at any time of the year, even in winter if the weather is warm, but their greatest activity is in spring and summer. Hot dry conditions, however, reduce their activity till it rains again.

Tick paralysis

Tick paralysis is most common in late winter and spring, though it can occur at any time of the year. Any stage of tick growth may be responsible, but adult females are the most likely cause, and their paralysis is usually most serious. Not every tick, however, causes paralysis and some dogs appear more susceptible than others. Small dogs, especially long-haired ones, seem most susceptible.

White-haired dogs are said to attract more ticks than darker coated ones. Short-haired retrievers, beagles, foxhounds, pointers and setters seem more resistant, though it may just be that ticks are more easily seen on these dogs and picked off early, so they develop a partial immunity. Immunity generally only lasts six months or so, and one attack won't necessarily give an animal immunity at all.

Ticks can roam around a dog or cat for a day before they attach themselves. Then, usually, at least four or five days elapse before symptoms show. These vary, but the first real sign is weakening of the back legs with loss of appetite, cough and respiratory trouble and then increasing paralysis. If the tick is pulled off before symptoms appear, they rarely develop.

Ticks on humans

The first sign of a human having been bitten by a tick is often a headache. Often the tick bite itself won't be felt, though the area around it may be swollen and numb.

Control

Search dogs' coats daily in tick-infested areas, particularly in spring and summer. Check head, neck and front legs especially, as well as between the toes, and in the nostrils, ears and lips. Ticks should be removed immediately. Grasp them between your thumb and forefinger and tug sharply. The whole tick should come out. If it doesn't, use a needle. If symptoms occur, get professional advice.

Repellents

If you live in a tick-infested area, the best prevention is bathing your pet in derris – 60 g of derris dust to 4 litres of water – or dusting the powder through their hair. This must be done every week to be effective, and re-applied after rain or swimming. Wash the animal thoroughly in warm water first. Derris is not poisonous to mammals but is deadly to fish. Don't let your dog bathe in the fish pond.

For a milder repellent, try combing equal parts of eucalyptus oil, pennyroyal oil, thyme oil and olive oil through pets' hair. If you can't get thyme oil, take a handful of thyme leaves and just cover them with hot olive oil. Leave for at least 24 hours. Renew this every week or so when the perfume is no longer noticeable.

Garlic taken internally is supposed to make animals less prone to ticks: at least four cloves a day chopped up in their food for a medium-sized dog. I don't know how effective this is, but it certainly has a wonderful effect on coats and general health. Frequent sea bathing is also reported to slightly lessen a dog's susceptibility to ticks.

People

Hazards of commercial pesticides

Deet (N, N-diethyl-m-toluamide) is banned in the USA. Prolonged use can affect the central nervous system. Never use products containing Deet on children.

Other repellents contain pyrethrum. This is safe to use on the skin, though an allergic reaction is possible – try a little first on your wrist. Synthetic pyrethroids are also safe to use.

Personal pest repellents

Pest repellents are probably as old as our ancestors' camp fires – smoky fires are an excellent way to keep pests from bugging you. Ashes rubbed into fat and plastered on your skin keep away midges and sandflies. A smouldering fire of old cow- or horse-manure is said to keep away mosquitoes. I haven't tried it. Like many pest repellents – including spray-on aerosols – many people would think that these ancient solutions are worse than the problem.

Nonetheless, many old-fashioned remedies work well. (Many, like citronella oil, aren't very effective at all.) Like many organic remedies, though, they are not marketed because they break down quickly, and so have a low shelf-life. With home-made pest repellents it's best to grow – and make – your own.

Natural general repellent

1 part methylated spirits
1 part lavender oil
1 part cider vinegar
1 part eucalyptus oil

Shake well. Dab on as needed.

Personal rub-on repellents

Many plant extracts repel insects. Some irritate the skin and should be avoided. Safe ones include nut grass oil (rub on the bulbs from the weed you dig up in the garden, or steep them in bland oil), stinking roger, citronella, pennyroyal oil, Huon pine oil. The easiest to obtain and most attractive repellent for most night-time pests is lavender oil rubbed on the skin.

All-purpose rub-on repellent – an alternative 'aeroguard'

Measure three tablespoons of brandy and three tablespoons of bland oil into a jar. Now add the crushed leaves or flowers of as many of the following as you can: eucalyptus leaves, lavender flowers, santolina leaves, pennyroyal leaves, native pennyroyal leaves, grey myrtle leaves, wormwood, basil, cedronella. Add a few drops of eucalyptus oil and about twice as much lavender oil. Leave on the window sill for three weeks, shaking every day.

All-purpose insect repellent candle

Melt three candles in a saucepan. Add a tablespoon eucalyptus oil, a tablespoon lavender oil, a tablespoon derris dust, a tablespoon of dried chopped wormwood (it should take about three days to dry in the sun or overnight in a warm oven) and a tablespoon of chopped dried lavender flowers to two tablespoons of dried chopped lavender leaves. You can also add a teaspoon of cedronella oil if you can find it.

Reform the candles as above. You will need to burn at least two, one on each side of you.

Herbal pest-repellent stick

2 tablespoons of beeswax
half a tablespoon of cocoa butter
1 tablespoon of cocoa oil (you can use two tablespoons of your
    preferred moisturiser if you prefer)
a teaspoon of lavender oil
3 teaspoons of eucalyptus oil
half a teaspoon of any other of the specific pest repellent oils
    mentioned in this book, according to which pest you most want
    to repel

Melt the beeswax in a glass jar standing in hot water. Mix in the rest. Pour into an empty deodorant case (or any other suitable container). Leave to set.

Elderflower water

This is an old gypsy remedy to keep off flies. Pour boiling water over elderflowers – just enough water to cover. Leave to cool and apply liberally. It has some effect, but won't make you fly-proof. Elderflower water is also reputed to help skin exposed to sunlight.

Flies

The most likely flies to cluster on your face and back are bush flies.

Eucalyptus oil is the best repellent for bush flies. I discovered this with an injured kangaroo – it continued to get fly-blown with every commercial repellent I could find – only eucalyptus oil kept it fly free. Mint, tansy and basil are supposed to repel flies. Tansy may irritate the skin, so use it with discretion. I've never found the other at all effective.

Pennyroyal oil – especially native pennyroyal oil – seems to be more effective, but not as good as eucalyptus. Bergamot oil has some effect. English gypsies used to make a tea of horehound and wash with it to keep away flies. Maybe English flies are less persistent than ours. I find the tea has a slight effect, but this vanishes quickly.

Stinking roger leaves can be crushed and rubbed on the skin to repel flies. It is very effective, but many people find the scent unpleasant, and many also find it irritates their skin or they are allergic to it. Stinking roger is a tall, yellow flowered weed with marigold like leaves.

Leeches

An old-fashioned leech repellent trick was to send a pet lamb in front of you in the bush. The leeches clung to the pet lamb.

There have been two commercial leech repellents I've been able to track down. One was organic, but neither worked; perhaps the leeches were just exceptionally hungry and I was the only prey around. They might perhaps be more effective in the bush if there are other people about who are not using repellents and could be preferred food. I also tried citronella oil and lavender oil. The leeches seemed confused and certainly took longer to attach themselves than the control leeches did elsewhere; but attach themselves they finally did. I finally tried 'Arpege' perfume – which worked best of all. In fact any strong scent helped a little. Perhaps, while bushwalking, that confusion might give you time to get out of their way – but there seems to be no completely effective leech repellent. Leeches are attracted to warmth, not scent.

Huon pine oil is an old-fashioned leech repellent. I have been unable to find any and haven't tried it. Aboriginal people in Western Australia used the cut bulbs of the giant waterlily rubbed on their skins to repel leeches. This is another remedy I haven't tried, but it is claimed to be effective.

An old bushwalking trick is to wear two pairs of socks, the outer layer thickly impregnated with salt. This again is a deterrent, but not completely leech-proof. Some people find a coating of soap works. It doesn't for me; but then, leeches seem to head for me in preference to any other blood supply. As a last resort, rubbing your skin with gum leaves seems to make it slightly more difficult for leeches to find you.

If leeches attach themselves to you, try rolling them quickly with the flat of your hand. They will disengage without tearing your flesh. Never just pull them off – the scar will be with you for years. Alternatively, hold a lighted match to the leech or sprinkle it with salt or vinegar.

Leeches prefer not to cross dry cement paving: it needs to be a couple of metres wide. Try also making barriers with dry ash; with salt in halved, black polythene pipe; with diatomite; or with sharp gritty sand.

I tried copper bands with slugs and as a last resort tried it with leeches. To my surprise it worked. Leeches do not like crossing copper. While a thin band of copper keeps away slugs, leeches can raise themselves up and 'hump' over copper. The bands need to be wide enough to stop a good-sized leech: about as wide as the length of your index finger. Otherwise, even a narrow strip of copper will deter leeches as they wave around trying to find out some way of avoiding it. A thin strip of copper on your boots should give you time to get away before the leech crawls up your leg.

Leech bites

Leech bites itch. Dab them with any alcohol: brandy, vodka, listerine, etc.

Midges

An old Aboriginal remedy against midges is a coating of sand and fat: possible if you're desperate at a barbecue at the beach. Otherwise, try lavender and other mosquito repellents.

Mosquitoes

Have you ever felt that mosquitoes prefer you to anyone else in the room? It may not be paranoia. Mosquitoes prefer female blondes, preferably plump ones – their attraction is linked to body warmth, hormones, the amount of perspiration, and where you are in your monthly cycle. The more attractive you are to mosquitoes the more repellent you'll have to rub on, and the more often you'll have to refresh it.

Lavender repels mosquitoes for about two hours in women and four hours in men. You should be able to smell it when it's rubbed on – if you can't rub on some more.

Cedronella or balm of Gilead will repel mosquitoes – rub the leaves on your skin or soak them in a little oil and brandy (half-and-half) for a few weeks, shaking every day. If you can grow grey myrtle, or *Backhousia myrtifolia* you can treat the leaves in the same way.

In Algeria, mimosa flowers (*Acacia farnesia*) was used both as a mosquito repellent (rubbed on the skin) and as an aphrodisiac (eaten). (Perhaps in Algeria keeping the mosquitoes away was enough of an aphrodisiac.)

Paperbark oil is an excellent mosquito repellent – steep the leaves in a bland oil on the window sill, shaking every day for three weeks. Unlike lavender oil, though, this oil will stain your clothes. Fresh or dried pennyroyal leaves repel mosquitoes, but not as effectively as the other repellents. Native pennyroyal appears to be more effective.

Mosquito-repellent candles

These candles will help keep away mosquitoes – but hot air rises, and you may find that even if the candles are by your feet the scent will only repel mosquitoes by your face.

Melt down a few candles. Add a slug of lavender oil to the wax – and if possible many dried, crumbled lavender flowers. These will splutter as they burn, but are even better than lavender oil, which doesn't mix well with candle wax. If you can't find lavender flowers the leaves will do as well – they aren't as strong though and you will need more. Make sure they are dry before you add them.

Re-form candles. If you don't have a candle mould just pour the wax in a saucer or a small can (tiny baked bean cans are excellent) and thread the wick round and round as it starts to set, leaving a little out of the middle.

The candles will splutter as they burn, but the scent is lovely enough to burn even when there aren't any mosquitoes.

Baby clothes

Add lavender oil to the final rinse for baby clothes – or sprinkle them with a few drops after they've dried. This will help keep mosquitoes away from the child.

Night-time pests

If you are planning to eat outside at night you have three choices: personal repellents, repellent candles, or an insect repellent light.

Insect repellent lights

A white or blue light (most fluorescent lights are blueish) attracts pests, while a redder light will not. If possible eat under a reddish light with another light some way off to attract pests.

We have made our own insect-trapping light – a bright fluorescent light in an old soft drink bottle. Whenever we have our soft reading light on we also turn on this light. The flies, moths and mosquitoes are attracted to the blueish light, and are trapped inside it – while we are unmolested a few metres away.

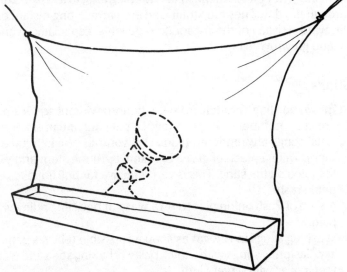

Place a gaslight, torch, or other electric light behind a sheet with a water-filled trough at its base. The light will attract insects which will fly against the sheet, then drop into the water.

Insect zappers

These work – killing large numbers of beneficial insects as well as pests. Avoid them.

Ultrasonic repellers

Ultrasonic repellers are supposed not to be heard by the human ear. They used to be used in the orchard industry to keep away birds – till after a few days pickers refused to go into the orchards where they were. Some people can hear them after three or four days; others can't – but complain of headaches and general unease. The sound may be above our threshold – but many people are still affected by it. So avoid them. As with insect zappers, who wants to live in a human desert, without other species around? Insect species are the most common animals around us. Why destroy them unless they are actively doing us harm? Stick to specific repellents, and avoid the ones that work on everything.

Sandflies

The term sandflies is used to apply to several small biting flies. *Ceratopogonid* sandflies are probably the most common sandflies to annoy humans, prevalent in coastal and mangrove areas as well as inland. They bite at night, in the morning and, to a lesser extent, through the day. They are small, and are carried long distances in the wind. Try any of the mosquito repellents, especially lavender oil and grey myrtle oil.

Stings

Remove the sting carefully from the bottom without squeezing it. There are a number of ways to reduce pain and inflammation.

- Ants' stings are rendered painless if you rub bracken juice on them. Take a piece of green bracken, twist the stem and wipe the juice on the sting. This is very effective for bull ant bites and nettle rash.
- A slice of fresh onion placed on a wasp or bee sting relieves the pain.
- Washing stings in vinegar as soon as possible relieves pain.
- Try plastering stings with a thick paste of baking soda and water, then cover with a wet cloth.
- Rub the leaves of large plantain (plantain major) on stings and nettle rash.

- Rub savoury leaves on bee stings.
- Rub on the fresh gel squeezed from aloe vera leaves.
- Apply crushed St John's wort leaves.
- Rub on crushed calendula flowers.
- Rub on bruised plantain leaves.
- Rub on bruised pennyroyal leaves.

If no other remedy is available, keep the stung area cool: with ice if possible, or cold water, a wet hanky or even mud. Alcohol, such as brandy or Listerine, will evaporate, leaving the area cooler. This will help relieve pain and itching, and possibly inflammation.

Cornflour tea

This tea soothes itching bites. Cover cornflowers with a little boiling water. Dab on bites when cool.

CHAPTER 3

Recipes

You can either grow the ingredients mentioned in these recipes (see Chapter 4) or buy them. Many are available as 'teas' for human consumption from health food stores. Soap can be added to all recipes as a 'sticking' agent, but sprays and washes will keep better without it.

Please remember that there are a number of basic rules you should bear in mind.

Avoid pesticides – even organic ones – if you can. Pests are food for their predators. A small pest population in your garden, for example, may mean a predator population ready to expand if seasonal conditions cause a pest population explosion. Most pesticides kill at least some predators too. Any pest will have something that feeds upon it, and should be encouraged to do so.

Even organic pesticides may be poisonous, though most of the ones in this book are not. Assume, however, that any pesticide is poisonous. Label them POISON, keep out of reach of children and try not to store them.

Organic pesticides break down quickly. This means they must be re-applied. Don't assume they don't work because the area gets re-infested. Combine any pesticide use with a sound management technique for getting rid of the pests.

Use traps, barriers, good management, general hygiene if appropriate, before you resort to pesticides. Use the most specific ones first, then the less powerful, gradually moving up to derris and pyrethrum and – as a last resort – nicotine.

Never leave any pesticide in reach of children or animals or in unlabelled bottles, old soft drink bottles, etc. To be safe, always make your brews and use them when fresh. Even organic remedies that break down quickly may be toxic to some degree and can often be highly toxic, if only for short periods.

Household pests

Sprays

Derris spray

This is an effective general insecticide for home and garden use. It is also known as rotenone. It causes minimal harm to humans in normal household doses. It breaks down under sunlight in a few days, but it is longer lasting than pyrethrum. It is not very toxic to predators but deadly to fish, so keep it away from dams and fish ponds. It is also toxic to caterpillars and some soil microflora. It is not an effective contact poison: it works best when eaten, so is most effective on leaf eaters or left for some time to work.

Derris is usually sold as a powder and should be available wherever garden supplies are sold. It can also be mixed as a spray or a wash or mixed with talcum powder or flour for use on animals. Used this way, it is a very effective flea killer.

120 g soap
4 1/2 litres water
60 g derris powder mixed in another 4 1/2 litres water

Mix all ingredients and dilute in another 12 litres of water. Mix again and use. This may separate out and need re-mixing.

For a simpler recipe use 1 kg derris powder with 1 kg pure soap powder. Mix with 20 litres of water.

Feverfew spray

Feverfew flowers are often mistakenly called pyrethrum in the garden. They aren't, but they can be used in the same way. Simply double the quantity of flowers used. Feverfew flowers are not poisonous and they can be used to make a mildly sedative tea that is good for headaches, including migraines. See 'Pyrethrum spray'.

Fly spray: see 'Pyrethrum spray'.

Garlic spray

This is not poisonous to humans or pets. It is also not very effective.

85 g garlic, unpeeled
2 tablespoons mineral oil
600 mL water in which 7 g soap has been dissolved (or as soapy a solution as you can make).

Soak the garlic in the oil for 24 hours. Add the soapy water. Strain and store in glass, not metal, away from light. Dilute with 10 times the amount of water to begin with; then make it stronger if it isn't effective. The smell isn't as bad as you would expect and doesn't linger when sprayed.

Pyrethrum spray or lotion

Pyrethrum spray can be used as fly, flea or plant spray. It is a broad-spectrum spray. It will kill some predators, but it has low toxicity for humans and animals. It breaks down in sunlight in anything from two hours to two days. Spray it at night outdoors so it doesn't affect bees and other useful species. Commercial pyrethrum sprays are available. Check the contents carefully. Many are made from synthetic pyrethrums.

Remember, like all organic sprays, pyrethrum breaks down quickly. If you spray pyrethrum one day and have pests again a week later, don't blame the pyrethrum. It probably killed them but more pests moved in. Organic remedies should only be used in conjunction with preventive measures.

Pyrethrum spray or dust may be made from pulverised pyrethrum flowers (*Tanacetum cinerariifolium*) or from feverfew flowers (*Tanacetum parthenium*), often incorrectly called pyrethrum. They have the same effect.

1 tablespoon pyrethrum powder
or 2 tablespoons flowers
or 4 tablespoons feverfew flowers

Cover flowers with alcohol (like brandy or sherry) or mineral oil overnight, then cover with one litre of hot water for an hour. Soapy water is best but not necessary. It helps the spray stick on the plant. Strain and use. Never boil pyrethrum: the fumes are toxic. Pyrethrum spray has about a 12-hour toxicity. It can be stored for a few days in a cool dark place.

Quassia spray

This is a weak general insecticide. It is an old-fashioned nit remover. A pyrethrum lotion is more effective.

60 g quassia-wood chips
8 litres water

Boil the chips for two hours. Strain. Add enough soap to make it lather. Spray.

Tansy spray

Tansy inhibits feeding. Cover 1 cup chopped tansy with 2 cups hot water. Cool. Strain. Spray.

Wormwood spray

This both kills and repels fleas and other pests like flies, moths, and mosquitoes.

Cover leaves with boiling water and leave for three hours. Dilute with four parts water.

Baits

Jam bait

Combine equal parts of jam and derris dust, or equal parts borax and jam. Place these in a jar with the lid on which has a small hole to let ants in.

Protein bait

1 part peanut butter
1 part cooking oil
1 part borax

Mix well. Place the bait in a plastic bag and cut a tiny hole in one corner to allow the ants or other pests access and keep the bait away from pets and children. This bait should last for about three weeks.

Wet bait

1 cup water
1 cup sugar
4 level teaspoons boric acid or borax

Stir until dissolved, then pour into a glass jar loosely filled with cottonwool. Put the lid on and punch holes in it. Leave near ant trails.

Oils

Kerosene oil emulsion

500 mL water
quarter cup of kerosene
quarter cup of liquid detergent
4 dessertspoons of vegetable oil

Mix well. This can be poured in ants' nests to destroy them or sprayed on ants.

Repellents

Diatomaceous earth

This is made from finely-ground marine skeletons of diatoms, one-celled shelled creatures. The microscopic needles of shell puncture the insects' bodies or grind their carapaces. The pests die of dehydration. It should be dusted on plants for caterpillars, thrips, mites, slugs, snails, heloianthis caterpillar, and pear and cherry slug. It will seep into the carapaces of cockroaches and silverfish and deter or eventually kill them.

Cover your nose and mouth with a hanky when dusting diatomaceous earth as it can be irritating if inhaled.

Fly repellent

This is suitable for humans or can be brushed through an animal's hair.

Mix:

3 parts oil of cloves
5 parts bay tree oil
5 parts eucalyptus oil
150 parts alcohol (this can be brandy)
200 parts water

Fly, mosquito, sandfly repellent

1 part methylated spirits
1 part cider vinegar
1 part eucalyptus oil

Place in a bottle. Shake well. Use as needed.

General insect repellent herb sachet

Pick any of the following:

any mint (native mint, spearmint, peppermint, pennyroyal, eau de cologne mint, etc.)
rosemary
summer or winter savoury
lemon or lime verbena
any of the lavenders
santolina (cotton lavender) or sea lavender (yellow flowered santolina)
basil (any of the basils)
thyme (any of the thymes, though common bush thyme is probably the strongest)
marjoram or oregano
caraway

Dry the herbs in a cool oven or in the sun. Make sure they don't get damp at dusk. Sew them into sachets and place in drawers.

Savoury sachet

Dry any of the following and sew into sachets or fold in old pillow cases:

bay leaves
garlic
lavender
orange or lemon rind
wormwood
mint
cloves
caraway
dill
lavender
woodruff
verbena leaves

Sweet spiced moth repellent sachet

Mix in equal parts by volume (e.g. half a cup each) of:

cloves
nutmeg
mace
cinnamon
caraway seeds
lavender

Now add the same quantity of ground orris root. This can be bought ready packaged from health food stores. If you have three cups of mixture, add three cups of orris root. This is a 'fixative'. Mix well. Sew the mixture into sachets – silk or old brocade is wonderful but an old sheet will do – and place in cupboards or drawers. If you can't find any orris root, make the mixture anyway; just be prepared to renew the mixture sooner when it loses its fragrance.

Plant pest sprays

Azalea spray

Take equal parts garlic spray, chamomile tea and nettle tea. Spray thoroughly once a week; include the underside of the leaves.

Bug juice

Mash one part pests with an equal quantity of water. Small pests may have leaves attached. Remember this when diluting and allow for this. Mix 1/2 teaspoon with 20 litres of water.

Clay spray

A dilute solution of clay – just add water till you can spray it – can be used over aphids and caterpillars. It is more effective on the former. It has no residual effect, of course, and must be repeated every couple of days till the predators increase and start controlling the aphids instead.

Coriander oil

Two parts coriander oil to 100 parts water, well shaken to an emulsion, can be used for red spider mite.

Coriander spray

This is effective against red spider and woolly aphids. Boil one part coriander leaves in one part water for 10 minutes. Strain and spray. This can also be used with anise.

Dipel

This is the commercial spray *Bacillus thuringiensis*, a form of bacterial warfare against caterpillars. It is extremely effective, though you must be patient and wait for the pests to sicken and die.

You can use Dipel to make your own culture. Gather a cupful of caterpillars from an area that has been sprayed with Dipel four days earlier. Mash them up and place them with three cups of milk warmed to body temperature, so it is neither hot nor cold when you dip your finger in it. Cover, and leave in a warm place (not hot) for three days. Strain. Add eight times the amount of water and spray. A little of the milk mixture can be saved as a starter for the next lot, or gather more infected caterpillars.

Glue spray

A weak solution of water-soluble glue will suffocate many small insects and their eggs, particularly aphids and thrips. It flakes off when dry. Flour and water glue can be made for this purpose.

Insect repellent spray

Blend together a mixture of:

garlic
onion
lavender leaves or flowers
mints
yarrow

Add just enough water to ensure even blending. Let stand for 24 hours at room temperature in a closed container. Filter. Add a few drops of detergent to help sticking. Add an equal quantity of water and spray onto plants.

OR

Take as many of the following as possible, chop them finely, and cover with water till it all ferments:
any of the mints
onion
garlic
spring onion
horseradish leaves or roots
red pepper
mustard
lavender
rosemary
wormwood

A pinch of yeast will help this along. Strain off the liquid and add four parts water and spray over any pest-infected plant.

Lantana spray
This is effective against aphids.

Boil 500 g leaves in a litre of water. Strain and spray.

Milk spray
This is effective against red spider mites.

1/2 cup of buttermilk
4 cups of flour
20 litres of water

Mix the buttermilk with the flour and then add the water. Spray every two days till mites are dead.

Mustard spray

This can be used to control scale. Take one part ground mustard seeds and add 20 parts of water. Spray. This is a very rough guide only and you may be able to dilute the mixture much more.

Oil spray

Oil sprays work by covering insects or their eggs with a light film of suffocating oil, especially in winter when the outsides of the eggs are more porous. But beware: oil sprays cause leaf damage in temperatures over about 24°C.

1 kg soap
8 litres oil

Combine soap and oil. Boil and stir vigorously till it dissolves. Dilute with 20 times the volume of water. This spray separates quickly so don't store once it has been mixed with water.

Onion spray

This is good against scale, thrips, aphids and mites.

1/2 litre boiling water
1 kg chopped, unpeeled onions
20 litres water

Pour boiling water over onions. Strain. Dilute with water. Spray every 10 days till pests are gone.

Onion garlic spray

This spray is effective against any leaf-eating insect, and has a limited effectiveness on most scale and hard-surfaced pests like shield bugs. Try this before you use anything stronger.

4 of the hottest chillies you can get
4 large onions
2 bulbs of garlic
2 litres of water

Combine the ingredients and cover with soapy water. Leave 24 hours. Strain. Add water and spray. Store in a sealed container in a dark place up to two weeks if necessary.

Pepper

Dust white or black pepper over caterpillars. It can also be used to keep away possums. You can make your own red pepper by growing the hottest chillies possible, drying them and grinding them to powder. The hotter the pepper the more effective the control.

Pyrethrum spray

See page 101.

Rhubarb spray

This is poisonous. It is also harmless to bees and breaks down quickly.

1 kg rhubarb leaves
3 litres water

Boil the leaves in the water for half an hour. Add enough soap to colour, and dilute with equal proportions of water before spraying. Keep out of the reach of children and label POISON.

Ryania spray

This is hard to find in Australia and usually expensive. Though it is very successful overseas with a wide range of caterpillars and beetles, including codlin moth, it is less effective in the hotter, more arid Australian conditions. It is harmless to most but not all common predators.

1 kg ryania powder
100 litres soapy water

Mix the powder with the water. Spray every 10 to 14 days.

Sugar spray

Dissolve 2 kg sugar in a bucket of water. Drench the soil to kill nematodes. Molasses can also be used but don't use honey as it may transmit disease to bees.

Stinging nettle spray

Cover nettles with water, leave for three weeks or until the liquid is pale brown to green. This can be diluted with two parts water and used for aphids. It is also a valuable foliar fertiliser and an excellent tonic for your plants. Use it freely.

Wormwood spray

This both kills and repels fleas and other pests like flies, moths and mosquitoes. It is effective against aphids, and deters snails if sprayed around seedlings. Cover leaves with boiling water and leave for three hours. Dilute, using one part spray to four of water.

Fungal and bacterial plant conditions

Baking soda spray

This spray is not strictly organic. Use instead of bordeaux: it is slightly easier to make. Never use on foliage.

100 g of washing soda
50 g soft soap
2 litres water

Mix together the washing soda and the soap. Dilute with water.

Bordeaux mixture

This is the standard organic fungicide. Always make bordeaux mixture yourself. It doesn't keep, and commercial mixtures aren't traditional bordeaux. Always use bordeaux within an hour of making it or it will start to separate. Try not to use bordeaux often. Use the other 'softer' fungicides first. Too much copper can affect soil fungi (high humus levels can mitigate this) and may also kill predators. If you have trouble with scale in spring and have been spraying with bordeaux, this may be the reason. Try spraying every second bush, then spraying the rest ten days later so you still have a nucleus of predators for when pests start to build up.

90 g of blue copper sulphate
4.5 litres cold water
125 g of slaked lime (brickies' lime not agricultural lime)
another 4.5 litres cold water in a non-metallic container

Mix the copper sulphate with the water in a non-metallic container. In a second non-metallic container mix the lime with the remaining water. Mix the two together. Stir well. Test with an old nail. Dip it in the mixture for 30 seconds. If it comes out blue you need more lime – or more mixing to dissolve the lime. Don't use it till you have corrected the problem, or you may burn your plants. Use within an hour, stirring occasionally. Use it with any spraying equipment, but have some water around to wash out the nozzles to stop clogging.

Bordeaux paste

This is useful for collar rot and tree wounds.

60 g copper sulphate

2 litres water
120 g brickies' lime mixed in 2 litres water

Dissolve the copper sulphate in the water. Add the combined lime and water. A tablespoon of powdered skim milk can also be added to this mixture to increase its effectiveness.

Chamomile tea

This is a very mild fungicide. Cover a handful of flowers with boiling water, or use a teabag according to instructions on the packet. Spray when cool.

Chive tea

This tea can be used against apple scab or powdery mildew. Cover chopped chives with boiling water: just enough to cover them. Infuse for 15 minutes and use undiluted.

Condy's crystals

Use this for powdery mildew.

7 g potassium permanganate (Condy's crystals)
7 litres of water

Combine ingredients and spray at once.

Elder spray

This works for mildews, black spot and a range of fungi. It is also poisonous. Boil 500 g elder leaves in a litre of water for an hour with lid on the pan. Top up with water as necessary. Strain and spray. This can be kept in a sealed bottle in a dark place for up to three months.

Esquisetum or horsetail spray

This is a mildly preventive measure, usually not a cure. It does have limited effectiveness, however, when symptoms first appear – especially on powdery mildew – and you cut off all infected leaves, this may stop the infection spreading. It should be sprayed fortnightly. Boil 20 g of esquisetum leaves (most health food stores have them) with one litre of water for half an hour. Strain and spray. Use at the rate of one litre to cover an area of 10 metres by 10 metres for the first spray, then dilute with 50 per cent more water for subsequent sprays. You won't get better control spraying more heavily: it is a homeopathic spray.

Garlic spray

Garlic spray is an effective fungicide. Unfortunately it also kills insects and should be used with discretion. It is very effective against brown rot, and can be sprayed on fruit after it has been picked. For recipe, see under 'Household sprays'.

Horseradish spray

Chop horseradish leaves, cover with boiling water, leave till cool and spray undiluted for any fungal problems.

Milk spray

Milk is effective against a range of mildews. Spray equal parts of milk and water every few days till the condition is cleared.

Mustard seed powder

Grind mustard seeds to a fine powder. Dust over plants affected by powdery mildew.

Nettle tea

This tea can be used against powdery mildew. It is also effective against aphids. Take a container of nettles, cover with water and leave for three weeks or till the water is mid-brown. Spray undiluted.

Seaweed spray

Wash salt from seaweed, cover with water for three weeks. Strain off as much water as you need, dilute till it is the colour of weak tea, and spray. This will strengthen a plant's resistance to a range of infections. It is also a mild fungicide and repeated use should cut down brown rot, curly leaf, and other such problems. It can be used at any time of the year, but spray at night in hot weather.

Urine

Don't shudder. Human urine is very effective against a range of mildews as well as apple and bear scab. Urine is sterile unless the donor has a urinary tract infection. It doesn't remain sterile when stored, and will develop a strong odour. Most people find the smell of other people's urine more offensive than their own. If you decide to use it, use it fresh.

Washing soda spray

Use this for downy mildew.

100 g washing soda
5 litres cold water
50 g soft soap

Dissolve washing soda in water. Add soap and use at once.

Pets' pests: remedies

Derris and eucalyptus lotion

Take 500 g of powdered derris, half a cup of eucalyptus oil and enough brandy or pure alcohol to make the whole just liquid. Allow to steep for three to four days, shaking twice a day. Now dilute with four parts water to every one part of lotion, and use.

If you need the lotion urgently, use it at once without waiting for it to steep. Then re-apply it four days later when it has been correctly prepared.

Derris powder steeped in methylated spirits and rubbed into the skin is an alternative to this lotion but not as effective.

Derris wash

This is a very effective flea killer. It does not have much residual action, however, and must be combined with treatment of the sleeping areas. For recipe, see 'Derris spray' under 'Household pests'.

Garlic and elder lotion

This is very effective lotion against mange. But take care, as it is poisonous and should only be used externally. Any treatment for mange requires careful attention to all areas of the animal: under the tail, between the toes. Anywhere left uncovered may be a source of further infection.

85 g garlic
2 tablespoons mineral oil
500 mL water in which 7 g soap has been dissolved
500 g elder leaves
1 litre water

Chop garlic. Don't bother to peel it. Soak in the mineral oil for 24 hours. Add soapy water. Strain and mix with three times the quantity of water. Now boil elder leaves in a litre of water for an hour with a lid on the pan. Top up with water as necessary. Strain and add to the garlic mixture. Use with discretion. This can be stored in a sealed bottle in a dark cupboard for three months. Mark POISON and keep out of the reach of children. If drunk, induce vomiting and seek medical advice.

Lemon peel lotion

This lotion is an old-fashioned remedy. Immerse squeezed lemon rinds in just enough water to cover them. Leave them till they are mouldy, squeeze them well, then replace with fresh squeezed lemon rinds as well as the juice from the second lot of lemons. Leave for three days, strain and then rub through fur.

Pyrethrum lotion

For recipe, see page 101.

Tea tree (Melaleuca alternifolia)

Tea tree oil is extracted from boiling the leaves and terminal branchlets and separating the oil from the condensed steam – 1 kilo of leaves gives between 12 and 25 g of oil. You can attempt an inefficient home version of this, but unfortunately the active ingredients in the oil appear to vary both from bush to bush and from area to area, and you may be unlucky with your cultivar. To be effective, tea tree oil needs a high terpinen-4-ol content, and a low cineole content (cineole is a skin irritant), and much of the tea tree in southern New South Wales often appears to lack these qualities.

Tea tree oil is an effective pest repellent – though no repellent will give 100 per cent control of a pest – and can be combed through dog's hair to repel fleas. It is also claimed to control nits (hair lice), and can be effective – it may or may not be as effective as commercial remedies. It is possible that the remedy merely makes it much easier to comb out the eggs. However, applying tea tree oil does destroy the eggs of many pests.

Tea tree oil is also bactericidal; it can penetrate unbroken skin and can be applied to pimples, boils, cuts, infected finger nails and insect bites; and it can be inhaled, mixed in hot water, if you have a cold.

Cultivation Melaleuca alternifolia prefers moist, swampy soil, but will grow in dryer conditions.

CHAPTER 4

Plants for Pest Control

Basil	Pennyroyal
Bay tree	Pyrethrum
Castor oil plant	Quassia
Cedronella or Balm of Gilead	Rosemary
Derris trifoliata	Rue
Eucalyptus	Sacred basil
Fennel	Santolina
Feverfew	Stinking roger
Garlic	Tansy
Hellebore or Christmas rose	Thyme
Horehound	Walnut
Lavender	White cedar
Mugwort	Woodruff
Nutgrass	Wormwood & Southernwood

BASIL

A pot of basil on the window sill is reputed to keep flies from the kitchen: one of the few herbs that repels without the leaves being crushed. Farmers' wives in some parts of France used to present each other with pots of basil to place on window ledges to keep away flies. In my kitchen the flies ignore it, but it's a wonderful herb anyway and I would rather give it the benefit of the doubt and hope it is at least cutting down the invasion.

Cultivation

Plant basil seed after frosts have finished, and keep it well fed and watered. Badly-fed basil is pale green with small leaves. Well-fed basil will grow to your knees. Beware of damping off in hot humid weather when the plants are young; drizzle the seedlings with chamomile tea. Make sure any organic matter in the soil is decomposed before you plant and that mulch is well parted till the stalks are older and tougher. Slugs and snails love basil. An oak leaf mulch will repel them as will sharp sand, a ring of salt in a halved stretch of pipe, a ring of copper, a spray of bordeaux mixture or nettle tea. Traps work well if you find the right bait: snails are conservative feeders and only like the sort of plant they have been dining on before. Try a halved, squeezed grapefruit, a dish of beer, a hollow raw potato or a cabbage leaf smeared with dripping. Empty beer cans make excellent snail traps: they shelter there and can be shaken out each morning and trodden on or fed to the chooks.

Basil grows easily from seed though it may take a few weeks to germinate. Try coating it in salad oil to prevent it rotting in cool weather before it germinates. It also readily takes from cuttings – which may be taken after Christmas – to propagate a new bush that is taken inside for winter. Keep basil well pruned to make it more leafy and to prevent it from flowering. In frost-free areas or on a warm window sill, basil may become perennial. Otherwise, cover leaves in olive oil for a basil fragrance in winter. A branch of basil was traditionally hung over the stove for ready plucking.

BAY TREE

Bay leaves can be used on bookshelves and in cupboards to repel silverfish. They can be placed in cereal storage areas to repel weevils. The leaves are fragrant dry or fresh, and can be used either way. Dry them slowly to retain colour and perfume. The bay tree was once thought to be sacred to Apollo, and explorers and games victors were crowned with it. The bay tree is also supposed to be resistant to lightning strikes.

Cultivation

The bay is an evergreen tree, well-shaped, dark green, growing from six to twenty metres. It grows slowly, especially when young, but once established it's drought resistant.

Bay trees can be cut by very heavy frost, but this is unlikely through most of Australia. If your tree is prone to frost, try mulching it heavily to protect the roots from freezing. Bay trees can also be grown in pots, which is a convenient way of keeping them near the house; but roots in pots are much more vulnerable to frost and heat. Place pots in a sheltered spot or wrap them well on cold nights.

Grow your bay tree from a cutting or a root cutting. Bay trees sucker freely, and many trees readily self-sow around the base from the small black fruit that follows the small yellow flowers.

A pale golden-leaved cultivar of the bay is sometimes available. The ones I have seen simply looked underfed.

CASTOR OIL PLANT

Powdered leaves have been marketed in the USA as an organic mosquito and general insect repellent.

Cultivation

Castor oil plant is a large, warm-climate shrub. It can grow to 8 metres under tropical conditions, but where it is cut back by frost or cold weather it will grow to about 2 metres in the first season and not grow much bigger. The leaves may have a reddish or purple tinge. The flowers are yellow, the fruits spiny. The seeds are large and marbled, and can be pressed for 'castor oil'.

The 'castor oil plant', *Fatsia japonica*, is sometimes sold as an indoor plant but it has no insecticidal properties that I know of.

CEDRONELLA OR BALM OF GILEAD

Cedronella is an excellent mosquito repellent and will also repel other insects.

Cultivation

Cedronella is a pink or blue-flowered herbaceous bush with ferny lemon-scented leaves. It grows up to 2 metres high, but often much less. It is wonderful in the garden as the leaves spread their scent for metres. Cedronella is slightly frost sensitive. It can be grown from seed or bought from herb nurseries.

DERRIS TRIFOLIATA

This native Australian derris grows in North Queensland. It is a vigorous rainforest creeper and climber, commonly growing near the shore, with trifoliate or pinnate leaves and flat kidney-shaped pods 3 to 5 cm long.

The dried pulverised root will provide a weak derris dust, though derris trifoliata is not the commercial derris dust.

Cultivation

Derris grows from seed, but I know of no commercial source. It is frost sensitive, and needs deep, good soil and moisture.

EUCALYPTUS

Some eucalypts produce far more oil than others. Around my house the narrow-leafed peppermint is most favoured for oil production, though any eucalypt can be used at a pinch. Test the oil content by crushing a leaf and smelling, or looking for the tiny oil globules on the leaf.

Small quantities of oil can be distilled by simply boiling the leaves in a large kettle (not one you will want soon for cooking) with the lid on. If the lid is off, the oil will evaporate. Attach an old hose to the spout. Collect the evaporated oil and water in a beaker. The oil will float to the top.

Cultivation

Different eucalyptus require different treatment. Ask at your local nursery for trees to suit your purpose. I prefer narrow leaf peppermint for eucalyptus oil, but there are many oil rich varieties.

FENNEL

Fennel is a flea repellent. It is the smell of fennel that is effective; there is no insecticide ingredient.

The enlarged leaf base of fennel can be eaten boiled, roasted, grated raw, or the stems can be stewed or pickled.

Cultivation

Fennel is a tall, hardy annual which can become perennial in mild areas, with green leaves and umbels of yellow flowers in summer. It likes a well-drained sunny position and may be propagated either by seeds or root division. Plant seeds in spring, and transplant about 30 cm apart. Don't plant fennel near dill as they cross-pollinate and the flavours may mingle.

Fennel leaves may be harvested at any time, preferably just before flowering. Fennel seeds may also be gathered when they are a grey-green colour. Both may be dried or used fresh.

FEVERFEW (*Tanacetum parthenium*)

Use feverfew whenever you would use pyrethrum, but make a stronger mixture. The strength of its active ingredients vary.

Cultivation

Feverfew is often incorrectly known as 'pyrethrum'. It has small, typical chrysanthemum-like leaves and white and yellow clusters of flowers. Once you grow feverfew you will always have it: it re-seeds readily. It can be either annual or perennial depending on climate. Sow seed at any non-frosty time.

GARLIC

Dried cloves of garlic will help keep weevils from food, and repel other pests. Dry the cloves very slowly in the oven. The dried cloves won't taint the food they are placed with. Garlic is a general insecticide and fungicide.

Cultivation

Garlic needs much the same conditions as onions: well-drained soil with decomposed organic matter. Too much fresh organic material means that the bulbs may rot. Heavy clay soils can cause misshapen, smaller bulbs. A temperature range of 13°C to 24°C during the growing season is perfect for garlic but if you mulch well and choose a sheltered site and don't mind smaller or discoloured bulbs you should be able to grow garlic in most of Australia.

Preparation

Garlic is shallow-rooted and needs good moisture while the bulb is forming. It also needs high levels of nitrogen and phosphorous. Like onions, garlic has limited foliage and so doesn't offer weeds much competition.

Planting

Garlic is grown by planting the cloves. Don't use a bulb that is partially rotten, and don't break them up before you are ready to plant – garlic lasts better whole. Garlic sometimes sets seed. Ignore it. It is almost certainly sterile. If your bulb is starting to shoot you can still plant the cloves – but the garlic will mature earlier, and be smaller and probably badly shaped. Don't use the small centre cloves – their bulbs will be smaller – and don't plant more than one in a hole or you may get small double plants. While small plants of other species don't matter, smaller garlic is a nuisance to peel: all skin and no substance. It is probably the one vegetable where large is better.

Garlic is mostly planted in autumn. This allows the plant to have the longest possible leaf-production stage before warmer temperatures start the bulb developing. The longer this cool period, the better the yield. In warm areas, chill garlic for 3 weeks before planting for larger, more even cloves. Plant early in autumn if you can, though winter-planted garlic (as long as the ground isn't frozen and the bulb rots before it starts to grow) will still produce a decent bulb. Even spring-planted garlic is better than no garlic. Summer-planted garlic goes mostly to leaf, and not all of it will germinate. Garlic germinates best at about 4.5°C, and while the soil temperature will probably be lower than that of the air, you may still have problems. If you do plant spring or summer garlic, do it in the coolest, semi-shaded spot in your garden, preferably with morning sun and afternoon shade. Mulch it well, preferably in an area that is already mulched so the soil is cooler. Never let garlic get too dry – or sodden. Garlic roots rarely go below 60 cm deep, so you only need water enough to soak to this depth. Any more wastes water and leaches nutrients. Light, frequent watering is best – again, unlike most vegetables.

Harvesting

Once the garlic tops start to yellow or droop, stop watering. Wet conditions at this stage can cause the bulb to rot if drainage isn't good, or can discolour the bulbs and make the outer cloves rot. Start pulling your garlic out when the tops have fallen over and are starting to dry. Don't leave it till it's quite dried off, unlike onions. If garlic is left too long in the ground, it becomes discoloured and the outer cloves may start to separate from the bulb, and so reduce the storage life. If you plant your garlic in autumn, you'll probably harvest it just before Christmas, though a hot spring may mean the bulbs mature faster. Cut off the tops about 3 cm from the bulb unless you want to leave the lot to make a garlic braid. Now leave the bulbs out to dry in the sun for an hour or so. Then let them finish drying either covered with a thin layer of dry grass clippings or something similar, to keep them from getting sunburnt and discoloured, or in a light airy shed if you think they might get rained on or damp from heavy dew.

Storage

Garlic stores well for at least three months, and for years if well dried and healthy. Garlic fertilised with decomposing organic matter generally lasts longer than garlic grown with artificial, high nitrogen fertilisers; but this also depends on how well it's dried. Hang it in open-mesh orange bags in a cool dry spot, or thread the bulbs on string and hang them under the verandah.

Problems

Garlic is reasonably trouble free. You may however be bothered by some of the following problems.

Thrips   These distort the leaves and cluster in the angles as the plant droops. Thrips are preyed on by a range of wasps, fungi, spiders, ladybirds and their larvae, and lacewings. Get rid of thrips with strong jets of water or spray with soapy water (not detergent) or, as a last resort, a derris spray.

Onion maggot   This may hollow out the stems. Make sure organic matter is well decomposed before you plant the garlic, or leave it on the surface where it belongs.

Downy mildew   This attacks the leaves, which turn yellow with a downy grey coating. It is worst in cool moist weather and if the garlic is planted too thickly. Try spraying the garlic with quarter-strength fresh urine and cut down on fertiliser. Otherwise, spray with chamomile or chive tea – made as you would to drink it – or boil casuarina needles in as much water as is needed to cover them for twenty minutes, strain and spray.

PERENNIAL GARLIC

I leave my garlic in the ground. In rare cases I dig it up and use a bulb but mostly I just use the tops: chopped up fresh in salads, simmered in stews, finely minced for garlic bread or garlic mayonnaise. By now the garlic is maturing every which way – there is nearly always some to harvest. The green tops aren't as strongly flavoured as the bulb – but they are easier.

HELLEBORE OR CHRISTMAS ROSE

The roots and leaves can be used as an insecticide. See the recipes used for derris in Chapter 3. Hellebore can be used where derris would be used and is reputed to be about the same strength. It is traditionally used for leaf-eating insects.

Cultivation

Hellebore is a winter flowerer, with dark green, thick leaves and white to pink to green flowers. They grow from seed if planted as soon as the seed is ripe; otherwise, divide old clumps.

HOREHOUND

English gypsies used to wash themselves with horehound water to repel flies and other insects. Horehound water can be made like any other tea. Simply pour boiling water over the leaves and leave to infuse for ten minutes.

Cultivation

Horehound is a woody perennial. It grows about 1 metre high, sometimes reaching 2 metres, in a sprawling bush with soft grey-green leaves. Horehound is a rampant grower and readily seeds itself and is a noxious weed in some parts of Australia. This, however, doesn't stop it being readily available in most nurseries. As long as you don't grow it where it can spread, horehound is a hardy and attractive garden plant. Sow at any non-frosty time of the year.

LAVENDER

Lavender is one of the most effective – and certainly most pleasantly perfumed – insect repellents. Rubbed on the skin, lavender oil will repel mosquitoes and other pests; strewn in cupboards it repels moths; around the house it repels carpet beetles, silverfish, etc.

English lavender (*Lavendula angustifolia*) contains the best quality essential oil of all the lavender varieties and the Tasmanian commercial lavender or Bridestow lavender appears to produce more than other cultivars. Cotton 'lavender' (see santolina) seems to be the most effective insect repellent, although it is not a true lavender. In the absence of sure labelling, test the lavender before you buy it by rubbing the foliage and then the flowers between your fingers, to test the intensity of the perfume. Buy the most fragrant.

Cultivation

Lavender can be grown from seed sown in spring. It takes about three weeks to germinate in warm soil. Otherwise, take cuttings in late autumn or early spring in cold areas. Press the woody stems at least one hand deep into the ground and keep moist. Most should take. Lavender is reasonably hardy and very drought tolerant, but may fail to grow in very exposed frosty areas.

Lavender also prefers alkaline soils and good drainage, though the rampant French lavender (*dentata*) and allardi lavender will tolerate almost any conditions, growing about a metre high and sprawling in all directions. Dwarf lavenders are wonderful, compact and fragrant. Green lavender seems to be the fastest-growing lavender but not as long living or fragrant as the others nor as spectacular, though the soft, fat, green flower heads are attractive close up.

Regular pruning will not only keep your bushes in shape – and give you the material for insect repellents and potpourri etc. – but also stop the lavender stems breaking down as they grow more woody and brittle and the weight of growth strains them.

English lavender takes about three weeks to dry. Pick it, string it in bunches and hang it upside down in a covered but light place like the verandah. French lavender can dry in two to three days or even in one very hot day.

All parts of the lavender bush are fragrant but the most perfumed are the flowers that contain the essential oil. Use the flowers if possible in potpourri and moth-repellent sachets, with or without the leaves. The leaves by themselves can be used as moth repellents. A home-made lavender-scented oil can be made by bruising the flowers to help release the oils and then covering them with olive oil in a sealed container for three weeks. Leave in a warm place like the window sill, or even heat slightly, making sure the pot is covered so the oil doesn't evaporate. If the oil isn't fragrant in three weeks, add more bruised lavender flowers and try again. Use the oil as an insect repellent either around the house or rubbed on the skin. You'll also find it soothes aching joints and muscles. Add a few drops of lavender oil to your furniture polish. Scatter a few drops in your bath.

Lavender wood can be made by taking neat bits of wood – wooden balls look best but don't use painted or varnished beads – and soaking them in the lavender oil for a week. Make sure the wood is completely dry first. Driftwood, well bleached, seems to absorb most oil. Take the wood out, dry well to take off the excess oil, then leave in your cupboards to repel moths or hang on the wall to scent the room. If you have very large pieces of driftwood, just rub them with the oil every day for a week.

Never use home-made lavender oil on carpets or clothes: it may stain. Pure distilled lavender oil, on the other hand, rarely leaves a mark on fabrics and can be spilt or spread with abandon. But test a little first to be sure.

Pick long branches of lavender, with or without flowers. tie them up at the base and hang them to repel clothes moths in wardrobes and weevils in the pantry. Lavender bunches hung over doorways and stoves will perfume the room – not strongly but just enough to give an almost unnoticeable welcoming fragrance.

MUGWORT

Mugwort will keep moths away in stored clothing or under carpets. It was once a favoured moth repellent but is not used much today as it is no longer popular as a garden herb. It was once used instead of hops to flavour beer.

Cultivation
Mugwort is a perennial herb. It grows to medium height and has a pleasant scent. The leaves are dark green on top and pale underneath. It has small flowers, either purple or yellow. Propagation is by cuttings or root division. It can also be grown from seed, and this is available commercially. Mugwort will grow anywhere. Pick the flower heads of mugwort just before they open and store them whole, or pick and dry the leaves at any time.

NUTGRASS

This is a common garden weed in warm areas, hard to eradicate because the 'nuts' underground allow the plant to re-grow if they aren't dug up as well as the plant.

Nutgrass oil is a southern Asian insect repellent, useful for flies, mosquitoes, bed bugs, etc. Almost cover the crushed stems or the nuts with safflower oil, and gently heat this with the lid on for an hour. Do not boil. Leave to cool, strain and use. Test on a sensitive part of your skin first to see if you react badly to it.

Cultivation
Find someone with nutgrass in their garden, and pull up a 'nut'. The owner will probably welcome you to it. Be careful. Once you have it, you may be stuck with it.

PENNYROYAL (*Mentha pulegium*)

Fresh or dried pennyroyal leaves or flowers can be used as a mosquito, flea, or ant repellent. Dried pennyroyal leaves can also be used scattered along bookcases to repel silverfish. It used to be known as 'flea mint'. Rats and mice dislike the odour of pennyroyal and it can be scattered wherever they may become a pest. It is excellent to plant around ant nests or in paving you wish to keep free of sandy ant mounds.

Cultivation

Pennyroyal is a hardy, low, prostrate plant with bright green leaves and purple flowers. It will grow in full sun, if well watered, or shade. Transplant runners, or sow in spring in a moist spot.

Native pennyroyal (*Mentha satureioides*)

This is claimed to be a more effective insect repellent than introduced pennyroyal. It will grow in dry rocky places as well as damp areas, unlike most mints. It can be found throughout mainland Australia.

PYRETHRUM, DALMATION PYRETHRUM

Pyrethrum is the source of the common, effective pyrethrum insecticide. It has a wide range of indoor and outdoor uses. Pyrethrum breaks down on contact with light. It is not toxic to pets and people, though some may have an allergic reaction. Test on the skin of your inner arm first, to see if a rash develops, before you use it widely.

Cultivation

Pyrethrum is not the ordinary white garden pyrethrum daisy. It is *Tanacetum cineraiifolium* and a common herb in nurseries in the last few years. It is low growing, to about 80 cm, with a bush of grey green leaves at the base and one flowerhead per stalk with yellow and white flowers in late spring/early autumn, though some ornamental cultivars are also sold. These too have insecticidal qualities, but they can be weak or variable.

Pyrethrum will tolerate growing in pots indoors near a well-lighted window or on the patio, and is fairly drought resistant. Pick the blooms for use in pyrethrum sprays or leave them to ornament the garden, where they will act as pest repellents next to vulnerable plants like cabbages. Pyrethrum is native to Yugoslavia but is now cultivated commercially in many parts of the world. Pick the flowers before they are fully open for the best effect. The flowers can be dried on sheets of newspaper in a well-ventilated place, then pulverised into a powder for flea powders, or made into pyrethrum spray.

QUASSIA

An infusion of quassia was the old-fashioned remedy against nits (the eggs of head lice) and pubic lice. It is also a general insecticide and a bird repellent for fruit. Quassia contains quassin, which has a very bitter taste. Hence its value as a bird repellent, as long as it doesn't rain.

Quassia used to be readily available from chemists but is now hard to come by. Commercially, it has been mixed with sugar to make fly papers. An old-fashioned fly spray was made by carving a quassia wood cup and leaving it full of water. This water, continually steeping till it turned yellow in the cup, was then used as an insecticide. Quassia chips are bitter to taste and have no smell. A quassia infusion is bright yellow and very bitter. Make a quassia infusion by steeping 30 g of quassia chips in 570 mL of cold water for two hours. Then strain and use.

Cultivation
Quassia wood is chipped from two trees: either Jamaican quassia from *Picrasma excelsa* or South American quassia from *Quassia amara*. The branches are cut, the bark removed and the white wood, which gradually turns yellow, is 'shaved'.

ROSEMARY

Rosemary can be used as a moth repellent in clothing, and added to sachets and potpourris.

Cultivation
Rosemary is an attractive greenish-blue, bushy shrub with blue, purple or white flowers. It likes well-drained soil and sunlight and will tolerate salty air. It may be grown from seed but can be slow to germinate and grow. It is best propagated from cuttings in

autumn or spring or from a root division. Rosemary is easily dried and retains its pungency. There is no need to dry it, however, before putting it in your cupboards. Just pick a branch and lay it under your clothes.

RUE

Rue can be used as a flea, cockroach or silverfish repellent, or added to potpourri or lavender bags to increase their insect repellent qualities. However, rue's perfume is hardly as pleasant as lavender and, in case you are sensitive to it, the plant should never actually touch clothing you will later wear. A border of rue in the garden may deter dogs and cats and occasionally less persistent wallabies and rabbits – but more often it won't.

Cultivation

Rue is a small shrub, with feathery blue-grey leaves and yellow flowers in summer. It can be grown from autumn cuttings, or from seed. Rue is slow to germinate. Leave seeds in hot water overnight, plant in spring and transplant as soon as it is big enough. It should grow about 2 metres high. It is perennial, evergreen and, apart from its odour if brushed, very attractive.

Treat full-grown rue with care. The important part for insecticides is the leaf with the active ingredient being rue oil. You might prefer to use gloves to pick it, as many people find their skins are sensitive to it. Never store it with clothes or near anything that will later touch your skin. Rue is most effective used fresh. The leaves lose some of their pungency when dried. If you need to dry rue, store it in an airtight container till needed and be prepared to use more for the same effect as fresh rue.

SACRED BASIL (*Ocimum sanctum*)

Sacred basil is native to Australia as well as much of South-East Asia. The fresh, crushed leaves can be rubbed on the skin as a mosquito repellent. Otherwise, the leaves can be used in the same way as pyrethrum flowers, although they are not as strong. To make an insecticide from sacred basil, crush the leaves and then pour on boiling water. Steep till the tea is a dark brown and use undiluted wherever pyrethrum would be used. Sacred basil is one of the sacred plants of the Hindus.

Cultivation
Sacred basil is a small-leaved, prostrate plant resembling marjoram. Treat it much the same way, though sacred basil prefers a more moist soil than marjoram. It is best grown from transplanted rootlets. It is frost tender.

SANTOLINA

Santolina is also known as cotton lavender. Like lavender, it is an effective insect repellent.

Both the flowers and the leaves can be used in the same way as lavender. Make santolina oil the same way as lavender oil. Unlike lavender, however, many people find santolina's strong perfume unpleasant.

Sea lavender is a yellow-flowered form of santolina and can be used in the same way.

Cultivation
Santolina likes hot, stony conditions but will grow anywhere in full sun. It is a small bush, up to 50 cm in height and about the same width, sometimes rounded sometimes sprawling, especially on a slope. It has thin grey-silver leaves and a woody base.

Santolina can be grown from seed, but strikes easily from hardwood cuttings taken in early autumn to early winter.

STINKING ROGER

Stinking roger is a weed. Tall (sometimes up to 2 metres), it grows readily on overgrazed country and has deeply divided leaves and small, long, yellow flowers. The leaves are particularly pungent when crushed, and on a hot day the plant can be smelled some distance away.

Stinking roger is an effective insect repellent. Traditionally it was hung in doorways to repel flies, and mattresses were stuffed with the dried leaves to repel bed bugs and other insects. The leaves can be rubbed fresh on the skin to repel flies and mosquitoes. This is effective but should be used with caution as many people are sensitive to it. Test a little first and keep away from the eyes.

Plant stinking roger around hen houses to keep away flies and lice. It can also be rubbed on animals to repel fleas. Both the flowers and leaves of stinking roger are effective, though the flowers are stronger. Try placing some stinking roger in a pan, pouring on enough boiling water to just cover it, placing a lid on and steeping till it is cold. Mix the resultant liquid with pyrethrum spray for a greater effect as a flea killer, or experiment with stinking roger tea by itself. Stinking roger can also be used as a companion plant to repel certain root-knot nematodes.

Cultivation

Stinking roger grows easily from seed, though you will have to collect this yourself. Plant it at any frost-free time. Stinking roger is an annual.

TANSY

Tansy repels fleas, ants, flies and other insects. It also kills insects and inhibits their feeding. It was one of the 'stewing herbs' of old England, used to keep away fleas and flies. It is especially effective as a fly repellent when mixed with crushed elder leaves. Tansy leaves can be used dry and sprinkled on window sills or shelves to deter ants, crumbled in dog bedding to repel fleas, or rubbed fresh through animals' coats to get rid of fleas. The leaves must always be bruised or crushed to release the insect-repelling oils.

Cultivation

Tansy is a perennial and a vigorous grower to about a metre high. It has green ferny leaves and bright yellow, button-sized flowers. These can also be dried and used in insect-repellent potpourri. They keep their bright colour for several years. Hang them upside down in bunches for a few weeks in a rain-proof spot with the leaves stripped off and only the flowers on the stalks.

Tansy grows best from a root cutting, taken any time of the year, in most parts of Australia, though autumn and spring cuttings take most easily. It can be bunged into any harsh, wet, dry, rocky or pure clay patch you have. Tansy leaves can be picked at any time of the year and are usually used fresh, not dried.

THYME

Thyme oil is a traditional lice killer (head and pubic) in human and animal hair. It can also be used for scabies. It is an extremely powerful antiseptic. There are over a hundred species of thyme all developed from wild thyme (*Thymus serphyllum*). It was used to fumigate ancient Greek temples, possibly an aromatic way of ridding them of fleas and other pests as well. Roman soldiers used to bathe in thyme water – ostensibly to give them courage but possibly also to get rid of lice which were as much a necessary accompaniment to soldiering as courage in those days.

Cultivation

Thyme can be grown from seed but usually is spread by root cuttings. The seeds don't grow true to type and thyme hybridises readily. It likes hot, dry-ish conditions but will grow even in semi-shade and moist soil. Choose a light soil if possible, though thyme is very adaptable. Don't ever fertilise thyme. At best it will become less perfumed; at worst it will lose its leaves, become thin and untidy or even die. Just let it grow. If your thyme is getting woody, or loses its perfume or vigour, top dress with compost to encourage new shoots along the stems. Thyme seems to lose its perfume after a few years if not pruned or divided. Harvest thyme preferably when it is flowering. At least two hard cuttings can be made every summer.

Caraway thyme is a low, spreading thyme with a strong caraway perfume.

Garden thyme is a clumpy, dark green bush with tough, woody stems. This is the 'herb stuffing' thyme and produces the best oil, though any thyme can be used. Its mauve flowers last through most of the summer.

Lawn thymes form mats. Their stalks are shorter and softer than bush thyme and the leaves are softer too so the thyme lawn is pleasant to walk or lie on and needs no mowing and almost no water. Lawn thyme grows rapidly, especially in hot conditions, and loves rockeries, paving and exposed areas. Lawn thyme can have white, cream or pink flowers.

Lemon thyme can be plain or variegated. It has pink flowers in summer and is vigorous, though not quite as drought hardy as garden thyme. It is probably the best thyme to attract bees. Thyme honey is loved by some people – not me.

Woolly thyme is less vigorous than the others, and is a soft-grey and furry.

WALNUT

Walnut leaves repel flies – if you have a lot of them. The trees are tall, spreading and drought resistant when established. Plant the trees in a grove, to shelter animals in summer and when giving birth or injured, or grow one near kennels or the kitchen window. Under a walnut tree is a good place for a chook yard. It will take several years of leaf litter, however, for the trees to have a fly-repellent effect. Collect the leaves in early summer, remove the stalks, and dry them quickly in the shade so they don't turn brown. Pour over boiling water to make a tea. Wash animals in this tea to repel flies, or soak bedding in it.

Cultivation

Walnuts are grown from seed, though named varieties are usually grafted onto them. Walnuts like deep, fertile, well-drained but moist soil. They are reasonably frost tolerant, and late flowering. Walnuts grow slowly but can become massive trees. Plant them with discretion in the home garden or cram them with other trees so they are stunned.

WHITE CEDAR (*Melia azedarach*)

White cedar leaves can be placed in books, on bookcases and in drawers to repel silverfish, in cupboards to repel moths and under carpets to repel carpet beetles. Crush the fruit, steep in just enough boiling water to cover them; when cool, brush through animals' coats to kill and repel fleas.

Warning: This is toxic. Never store, and keep out of the reach of children.

Make a moist poultice of the crushed flowers and apply it to chooks' legs to kill lice.

White cedar (*Thuya occidentalis*) is native to Canada and the USA where it is known as white cedar. It is called *Arbor vitae* in Europe. The plant is poisonous in large doses but has been used as a general insecticide.

Cultivation
Australian white cedar is an attractive garden tree, native to rainforests, grown in Queensland, the Northern Territory and the warmer parts of NSW. It has lilac flowers and poisonous yellow fruit. It prefers a deep, moist but well-drained soil with plenty of humus and a relatively frost-free spot.

WOODRUFF

This is a low, carpeting perennial with shiny leaves and small white flowers that stand out in a 'ruff' of leaves. Its scent is usually compared to new-mown hay. Woodruff was one of the classic old English 'strewing' herbs, mostly used to keep moths from linen, though also as an anti-flea herb strewn over floors. I don't know how effective it is as a flea repellent – I suspect it was scattered primarily for its perfume – but it does help keep away moths, and it perfumes stored clothes beautifully.

The leaves of woodruff should be picked just before or during flowering for greatest scent and effectiveness. The perfume becomes stronger as the plant wilts and dries. Dry woodruff at a low temperature so it retains scent and colour, and store it in an airtight container for later use if you don't want to use it at once with stored clothes or in potpourri.

Cultivation
Woodruff is a perennial, low growing and matting, preferring broken shade under trees and a moist, humus-rich soil. Woodruff seeds may take a long time to germinate and germination is often poor. The easiest way to propagate woodruff is to take a root division from an older plant and place it in a semi-shaded place, preferably under a tree, with a bare patch around where it can freely self-seed. Within a few years it should have carpeted the whole area.

WORMWOOD AND SOUTHERNWOOD

These are both artemisias, both powerful insect repellents. Wormwood is stronger than southernwood, and is used as an insecticide as well. Wormwood is essential for anyone interested in making their own insect repellents. It is a bitter, aromatic herb containing a volatile oil made up of various organic acids and a bitter glucocide, absinthe. There is a legend that wormwood sprang up around the Garden of Eden to prevent the serpent returning and that snakes avoid wormwood; unfortunately the snakes around here haven't heard the myth. However, dried wormwood and southernwood are effective moth and lice repellents. Bushes can be grown in hen houses to repel lice on chooks – the hens won't touch it – near the dog kennels and in the garden to repel pests like aphids, though the insect-repelling qualities are most effective when the leaves are moist.

Wormwood tea is an excellent insecticide for sap suckers. It is also an effective flea repellent: 'Where chamber is swept and wormwood is strewn/No flea for his life dare abide to be known.' (Thomas Tusser, circa 1532)

The active ingredients of wormwood come from the leaves and flower heads. Either can be used or, more traditionally, both at once. Pick the leaves and flower stalks just before or during flowering for best effect; though if needed they can be picked at any time. It can also be made into a home-made oil for combing through pets' hair to repel fleas.

Cultivation

Both wormwood and southernwood grow anywhere, under any conditions, though they grow best in reasonably fertile soil with occasional watering. They are hard to germinate. Be patient and accept that much of the seed probably isn't viable. They take easily from woody stem cuttings, however, taken preferably in late winter or early spring. Otherwise they will probably take at any time of the year except in frozen soil or full sunlight in midsummer. They are a perennial and evergreen except in very cold areas where they may lose their leaves in winter, then shoot again in spring.

INDEX

This index is additional to the table of contents, and the contents pages which begin each chapter. The discussion of a particular pest – ant, cockroach, mealy bug, etc. – in Chapters 1 and 2, will refer the reader to recipes for repellents, insecticides, etc. in Chapter 3, and to the relevant plants in Chapter 4. But the book is full of helpful suggestions which can only be appreciated by reading it from start to finish.

Other books by Jackie French

Organic Control of Common Weeds
Illustrated paperback, 128 pages
Recommended Retail Price **$13.95**

Natural Control of Garden Pests
Illustrated paperback, 160 pages
Recommended Retail Price **$15.95**

A-Z of Useful Plants
Illustrated paperback, 176 pages
Recommended Retail Price **$14.95**

Jackie French's Guide to Companion Planting
Illustrated paperback, 132 pages
Recommended Retail Price **$9.95**

New Plants from Old
Simple, natural, no-cost plant propagation
Illustrated paperback, 120 pages
Recommended Retail Price **$16.95**

Backyard Self-sufficiency
Illustrated paperback, 168 pages
Recommended Retail Price **$14.95**

The Wilderness Garden
Beyond Organic Gardening
Illustrated paperback, 192 pages
Recommended Retail Price **$19.95**

In Press (publication November 1993):
Jackie French's Chook Book
Illustrated paperback, 132 pages
Recommended Retail Price **$12.95**